EVERYTHING YOU NEED TO KNOW ABOUT

ENGLISH

HOMEWORK

Anne Zeman and Kate Kelly

An Irving Place Press Book

**SCHOLASTIC
REFERENCE**

New York   Toronto   London   Auckland   Sydney

Cover design, Charles Kreloff; Cover illustration, James Steinberg
Interior design, Bennett Gewirtz, Gewirtz Graphics, Inc.; Interior illustration, Moffit Cecil

For their assistance in the preparation of this manuscript, grateful acknowledgment to Betty Holmes, Director of UFT's Dial-A-Teacher, Barbara Mack, and Barbara Cook. Dial-A-Teacher is a collaborative program of the United Federation of Teachers and the New York City Board of Education. Thanks, also, to Margo Rudder of Irving, Texas, Kristin Marshall of Danvers, Illinois, Bill Johnson, and Wiley Blevins.

Illustrations copyright © 1995 by Scholastic Inc.

Library of Congress Cataloging-in-Publication Data

Zeman, Anne
        Everything you need to know about English homework /
Anne Zeman and Kate Kelly.
                p.   cm. — (Scholastic reference)
Includes index.
ISBN 0-590-49360-4 (hc)—ISBN 0-590-49361-2 (pbk.)
1. Language arts—Juvenile literature. 2. Homework—Juvenile literature.
[1. Language arts. 2. Homework.] I. Kelly, Kate. II. Title.
III. Series: Scholastic homework reference series.
LB1576.Z46 1994
372.6—dc20   93-46358
                                                                        CIP
                                                                        AC

14 13 12 11 10 9   0 1 2 3

                Printed in the U.S.A.   09

CONTENTS

Part 6. Creative Writing

Part 7. Practical Writing

Part 8. Reading Literature

Appendix: Some Good Books to Read

Index

It's homework time—but you have questions. Just how did your teacher ask you to do the assignment? You need help, but your parents are busy, and you can't reach your classmate on the phone. Where can you go for help?

What Questions Does This Book Answer?

In *Everything You Need to Know About English Homework*, you will find a wealth of information, including the answers to ten of the most commonly asked Language Arts homework questions.

1. What are homonyms, homophones, and antonyms? Homonyms, homophones, and homographs are defined on pages 25 and 26. A table of homonyms appears on pages 26-28. Antonyms are the subject of page 34.

2. How do you use a dictionary to find the meaning of a word? A guide to using a dictionary is found on pages 32-36.

3. How do you write a book report? A feature on book reports is found on page 105.

4. How do you find the main idea? The main idea of a paragraph is defined and illustrated on pages 64-65.

5. When and how do you use quotation marks? The proper use of quotation marks and other common punctuation marks is listed on pages 58-61.

6. How do you spell *exaggerate* and other difficult words? Commonly misspelled words are the subject of a table on page 25.

7. How do you write a poem? Guidelines for writing poems are found on page 89.

8. Where do you put an apostrophe to show possession? Find how apostrophes are used to show possession on page 58.

9. What is the difference between a simile and a metaphor? Simile and metaphor are defined on pages 78 and 80.

10. How do you form contractions? Contractions are defined and illustrated on page 31.

What Is the Scholastic Homework Reference Series?

The Scholastic Homework Reference Series is a set of unique reference resources written especially to answer the homework questions of fourth, fifth, and sixth graders. The series provides ready information to answer commonly asked homework questions in a variety of subjects. Here you'll find facts, charts, definitions, and explanations, complete with examples and illustrations that will supplement schoolwork colorfully, clearly—and comprehensively.

A Note to Parents

The information for the Scholastic Homework Reference Series was gathered from current textbooks, national curricula, and the invaluable assistance of the UFT Dial-A-Teacher staff. Dial-A-Teacher, a collaborative program of the United Federation of Teachers and the New York City Board of Education, is a telephone service available to elementary school students in New York City. Telephone lines are open during the school term from 4:00 to 7:00 P.M., Monday to Thursday, by dialing 212-777-3380. Because of Dial-A-Teacher's success in New York City, similar organizations have been established in other communities across the country. Check to see if there's a telephone homework service in your area.

It's important to support your children's efforts to do homework. Welcome their questions and see that they are equipped with a well-lighted desk or table, pencils, paper, and any other books or equipment—such as rulers, calculators, reference or text books, and so on—that they may need. You might also set aside a special time each day for doing homework, a time when you're available to answer questions that may arise. But don't do your children's homework for them. Remember, homework should create a bond between school and home. It is meant to enhance on a daily basis the lessons taught at school, and to promote good work and study habits. Although it is gratifying to have your children present flawless homework papers, the flawlessness should be a result of your children's explorations and efforts—not your own.

The Scholastic Homework Reference Series is designed to help your children complete their homework on their own to the best of their abilities. If they're stuck, you can use these books with them to find answers to troubling homework problems. And, remember, when the work is done—praise your children for a job well done.

EVERYTHING YOU NEED TO KNOW ABOUT

ENGLISH

HOMEWORK

LANGUAGES AND ALPHABETS

1 Languages

Languages Spoken Around the World

About 4,000 languages are spoken throughout the world today. Many of them are spoken by only a few people and within a small area.

Some people speak more than one language. In the United States, for example, many families come from other countries. Although these families learn English when they settle here, they may still speak the language of their home country. In some countries, people speak one language at home and another for business and politics. All people who can speak two languages are *bilingual*.

Today, English is often spoken in international business and politics. It is called an *international language*. For example, if a Japanese person wants to buy land from a person in Poland, unless they have an interpreter, the Japanese person and the Polish person will probably speak to each other in English. Spanish and French are two other international languages.

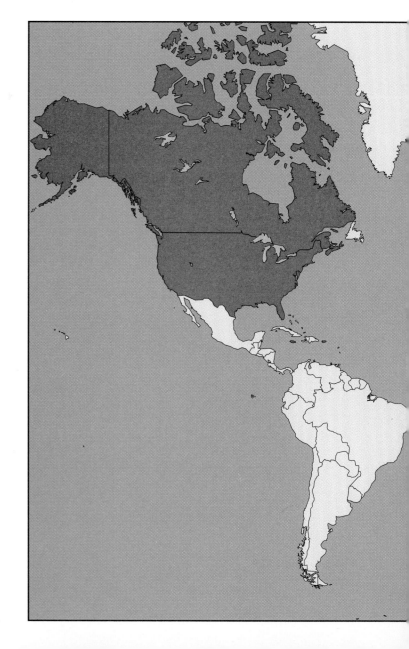

Places around the world where English is spoken are in red.

The World's MOST COMMONLY SPOKEN LANGUAGES

Language	Number of Speakers
Mandarin	over 1,000,000,000
English	475,000,000
Spanish	nearly 400,000,000
Hindi	nearly 435,000,000
Arabic	225,000,000
Russian	285,000,000

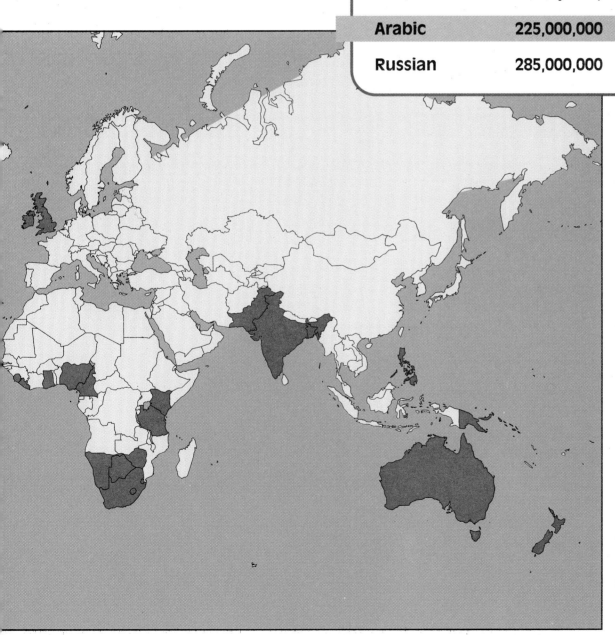

Indo-European Languages

The languages of the world are grouped into *families*. These families include languages that are related to each other. Most *linguists* (see p. 5) believe that the languages in each family grew out of one ancient language. English is part of the *Indo-European* language family.

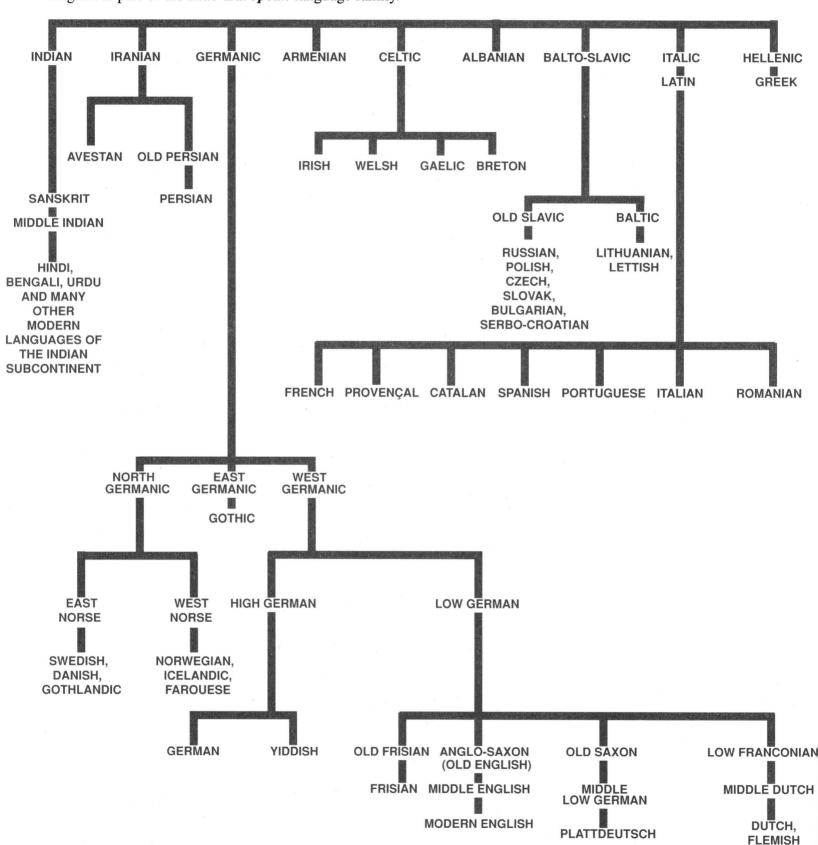

4

Here is the word *mother* in some Indo-European languages. Can you see
how they are related?

English	mother
Dutch	moeder
French	mère
German	mutter
Hindi	mata
Italian	madre
Spanish	madre

 *Some words are related through ancestral descent, derivation, or
borrowing. These words are called* cognates.

The Scientists of Language

The study of language is called *linguistics*. The people who study language are called
linguists. The different types of linguists include the following:

Grammarians. People who study *grammar*. Grammar means the parts of a language
and the rules for speaking and writing that language.

Phoneticians or phonetists. Those who study *phonetics.* Phonetics is the study of
sounds in speech. Phoneticians study how the tongue, lips, and teeth are positioned in order
to make different sounds. The study of speech sounds, *phonemics*, is part of phonetics.
When you study *phonics* in school, you are studying an area of phonetics.

Semanticians. Linguists who study *semantics*. Semantics is the study of the meanings
of sounds and words. *Morphemics*, the study of units of sound that carry meaning, is part
of semantics.

Morphologists. People who study *morphology*. Morphology is the study of how
language changes over time and in different places. For example, some morphologists are
concerned with the difference between Old English (used about 450–1100), Middle English
(used about 1100–1500), and Modern English (used today). Other morphologists are
concerned with the different ways the same language is spoken in different places. For
example, they might compare English in such countries as the United States, Canada, Great
Britain, and Australia, or Spanish in Spain, Mexico, and Peru.

Philologist. Those who study *philology*. Philology is the study of how the language of a
culture affects its literature.

2 Alphabets

A History of Our Alphabet

In English, we use a set of 26 letters to spell words:

A B C D E F G H I J K L M N O P Q R S T U V W X Y Z

This set of letters is our *alphabet*.

Our alphabet is called the Latin or Roman alphabet. Except for the letters *j*, *u*, and *w*, it was the alphabet used by the Romans 2,000 years ago. At first, the Roman alphabet had only 21 letters. Around 100 B.C., the letters *y* and *z* were added. *J*, *u*, and *w* were added much later to represent sounds spelled before with *y* and *v*, as well as to represent new sounds.

Where Did the Roman Alphabet Come from?

The Romans used the Etruscan alphabet to design their own alphabet. The Etruscans were people who lived in northern Italy about 8,000 years ago. The Etruscan alphabet grew out of the ancient Greek alphabet.

The ancient Greeks borrowed the alphabet of an even more ancient group of people, the Phoenicians. About 10,000 years ago, the Phoenicians lived in Byblos, a city in modern Lebanon. Byblos was a center for trading papyrus, a reed that was made into paperlike sheets of material. Our word *paper* comes from the word papyrus. The Greek word for book, *byblos*, comes from the name of the city Byblos. *Byblos* is also the root of our word *Bible*.

Phoenician

Early Greek	Later Greek	Roman	English
		A	A
		B	B
		CG	CG
		D	D
		E	E
		FV	F,U,V, W,Y
			Z
		H	H
			(Th)
		I	I,J
			K
		L	L
		M	M
		N	N
		O	O
		P	P
			(S)
		Q	Q
		R	R
		S	S
		T	T

HIEROGLYPHICS, PICTOGRAPHS, AND SYLLABARIES

Hieroglyphics are sets of special picture symbols used to write down stories or information. Among the best-known hieroglyphics are those used by the ancient Egyptians, who created an elaborate set of picture symbols to describe daily life, farming, and the wealth of pharaohs. Egyptian hieroglyphics are easy to recognize — but they are difficult to read. Reading hieroglyphics is so difficult, in fact, that the word *hieroglyphics* also means any handwriting, figures, codes, or characters that are hard to understand or decipher.

Pictographs are picture signs and symbols that tell a story, although the signs and symbols aren't organized into a set. The pictures drawn on cave walls by early humans are pictographs telling stories of daily life, hunting, fishing, gathering, and so on. Pictographs are still used today to chart information by using picture symbols to represent special kinds of information.

Syllabaries are sets of symbols. In a syllabary, each symbol represents a specific syllable that can be used in many different words. A syllabary was used instead of an alphabet in the writing systems of some ancient cultures and is still used today. The two sets of characters used in writing Japanese are modern examples of syllabaries.

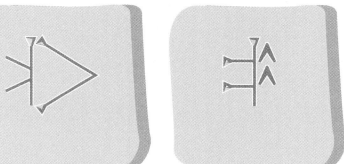

The early cuneiform symbol for an ox evolved from pictographs

Capital and Small Letters

Until about 200 years ago, only a small group of people could read and write. Some of these people, called *engravers*, cut (engraved) words and dates into stone tablets, or into the faces of buildings or monuments. The engravers used capital letters, which they carved in simple lines and curves into the stone.

Later, people called *scribes* were trained to write on papyrus and parchment. Papyrus and parchment were very expensive, so scribes had to fit as many words as they could on each precious page. Scribes also had to copy huge books such as the Bible, so they needed to write quickly.

Although capital letters were easy to engrave in stone, they were too large and difficult to form quickly when written with quill pens. So scribes developed *cursive* letters that flowed more easily together. At first, they rounded capital letters into *uncials.* By A.D. 1,000, they had created a version of the Roman alphabet in small letters. By combining cursive capital letters with small letters, scribes had a system of writing that saved space and time.

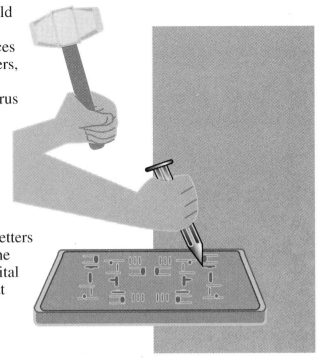

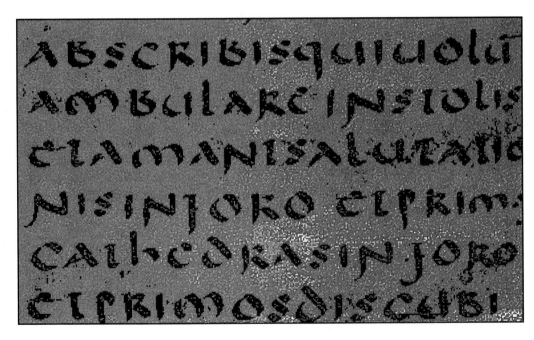

An early scribe wrote uncials on this sample of a manuscript created with ink on parchment.

Uppercase and Lowercase

Today we call capital letters *uppercase* letters. We call small letters *lowercase* letters. The terms *uppercase* and *lowercase* came about with the invention of printing presses.

Alphabet Spin-offs

Many alphabets are used in the world today. Some are closely related to the Roman alphabet. For example, the *Celtic alphabet* is still used in Ireland and Scotland to write the Gaelic language. The *Cyrillic alphabet* — used in Serbia, Bulgaria, the Ukraine, and Russia — was adapted from the Greek alphabet. The *Chinese* created an alphabet based on pictures called *characters*. The *Japanese and Korean alphabets* are based on characters, too.

Reading from Right to Left and Top to Bottom

Roman, *Greek*, and related alphabets are read from left to right. So is the *Hindi* alphabet, which is used in parts of India and Africa. But some alphabets, such as *Arabic* and *Hebrew*, are read from right to left. Still other alphabets, like the *Chinese*, are read from top to bottom.

Hebrew is read from right to left.

Chinese is read from top to bottom.

Sign and Symbol Languages

Sign Language

When people have difficulty hearing or cannot hear at all, spoken language is often not effective. **Sign language** was developed as another way of communicating for the hearing impaired. Signs that stand for letters and whole words are made by shaping the fingers and hands in different ways. People can have a conversation using sign language.

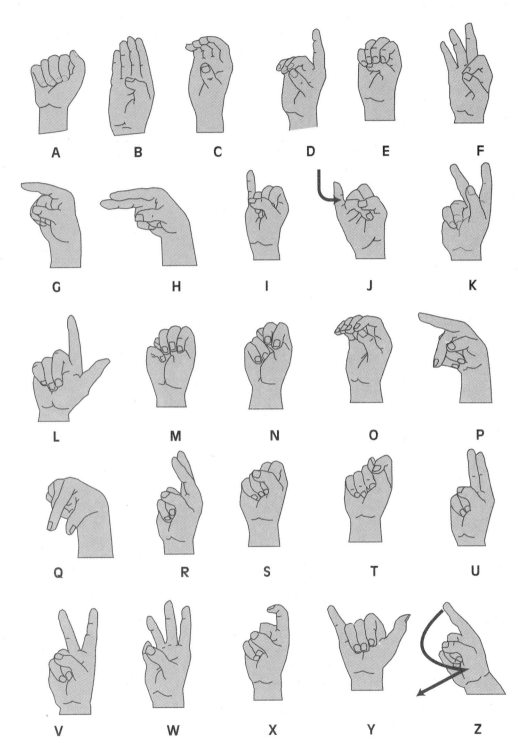

A B C D E F

G H I J K

L M N O P

Q R S T U

V W X Y Z

Braille

Reading words on a page can be difficult for people with poor eyesight and impossible for people who are blind. *Louis Braille*, himself a blind man, invented a special alphabet for people with sight problems in the late 1820s. The *Braille alphabet* consists of raised dots that are read by touch, not sight. Each letter has its own set of dots. The letters are written on paper held by a frame. The writer uses a pointed stick, or *stylus*, to make the dots. Today many blind people use machines similar to typewriters to make the dots.

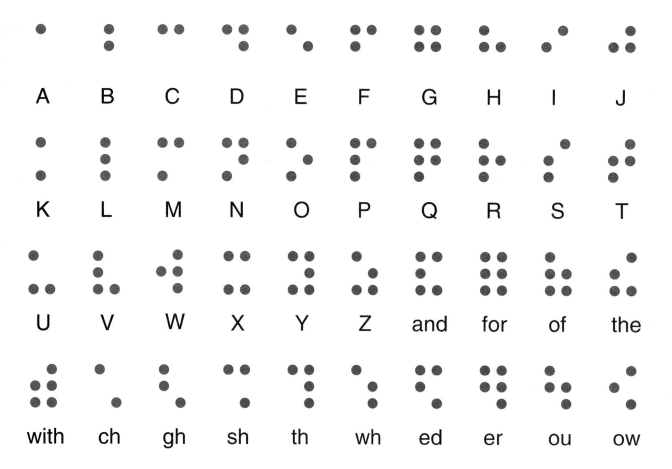

Native American Sign Language and Smoke Signals

Ancient Native American cultures, including the Mayas and Aztecs of Mexico and Central America, created writing systems made up of *glyphs*, or pictures. In North America, Sequoya, a Cherokee, invented a writing system made up of 86 signs that stood for the different sounds in the Cherokee language. But each tribe spoke a different language, so Native Americans from different tribes invented a simple sign language.

Native Americans on the Plains also communicated by smoke signals. The signals could be seen over many miles. By using smoke signals for basic communication, messengers were not needed to travel long distances over dangerous routes.

arrow   trade   friend

buffalo   horse   tepee

Native American   white person   peace

Semaphore

Sailors can't shout loudly enough over the noise of wind and waves to be heard on passing ships, and hand signs are impossible to read over the distances at sea. So sailors use *semaphore*. In semaphore, sailors use brightly colored flags in different patterns and angles to represent different letters and messages. The flags can easily be seen across the water.

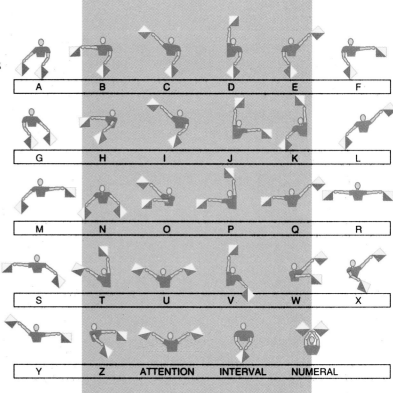

Morse Code

The telegraph was patented in 1837 by American artist *Samuel F. B. Morse*. In its day, the telegraph was the only machine that could send instant messages across long distances. It worked by sending messages in code through electric wires. The code, known as *Morse code*, consists of combinations of dots and dashes, which stand for the letters in the alphabet.

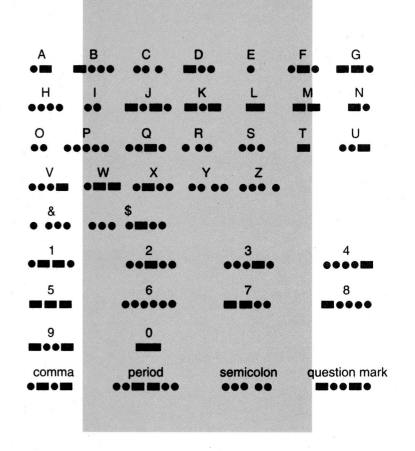

LETTER SOUNDS AND WORDS

1 Vowel and Consonant Sounds

Where Sounds Are Made

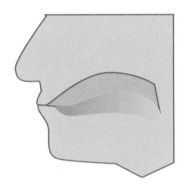

bilabial shape
(m,p,b,w)

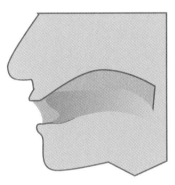

alveolar shape
(t,d,ch,j,n)

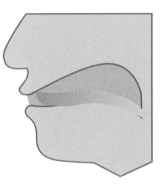

linguadental shape
(s,z,sh)

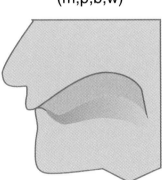

labiodental shape
(f,v)

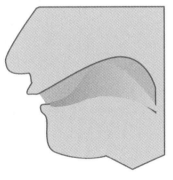

palatal shape
(y)

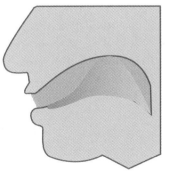

velar shape
(g,k)

Picture Keys to Vowel Sounds

Vowels	short		long	
a	apple	ă	angel	ā
e	elephant	ĕ	ear	ē
i	igloo	ĭ	ice	ī
o	octopus	ŏ	oak leaf	ō
u	umbrella	ŭ	universe	ū

Vowel Digraphs

Vowel digraphs are usually two vowels written together. Some stand for the sound of a long vowel (ai, ea, ie, oa). Others stand for new sounds (oi, ou, oo, au, ew).

ai, ay	**pain, say**		oi, oy	**boil, toy**
ea, ee	**bean, see**		ou, ow	**out, cow**
ie, igh	**tie, high**		oo	**boot, book (this digraph stands for two different sounds)**
oa, oe, ow	**boat, toe, snow**		au, aw	**sauce, claw**
			ew, ue	**grew, blue**

Other common vowel spelling patterns

ight	**height, night**
all	**ball**
alk, alt	**walk, salt**
ild, ind	**wild, find**
old	**told**
ear, eer	**fear, deer**

Blends

Blends are two or more consonants that keep their regular sounds when combined. Blends may appear at the beginning, middle, or end of words.

Some common beginning blends are bl, br, cl, cr, dr, fl, fr, gl, gr, pl, pr, sk, sl, sm, sn, st, and tr.

Some common ending blends are ft, mp, nd, and nt.

Sometimes when two or more consonants are written together they stand for a new sound. These blends are called *digraphs*

ch, tch	**chair, match**
sh	**ship, wish**
th	**thin, that (stands for two sounds—voiced and unvoiced)**
wh	**whale**
ph	**phone**

Sometimes when two or more consonants are written together, one of the letters is silent.

kn	**know**
wr	**write**
gn	**gnat**
mb	**comb**

Voiced and Unvoiced

Sounds can be *voiced* or *unvoiced.* A voiced sound is made by vibrating the vocal chords with air from the lungs. All vowels are voiced. Unvoiced sounds are made without vibrating the vocal chords, and often using the tongue and teeth. Many consonants are unvoiced.

Schwa

The *schwa* is the vowel sound heard in an unstressed syllable(´). The symbol for schwa looks like an upside down small *e.* Schwa sounds like a short *u* (u or uh). For example:

syllable = sil ə bəl

(See also Pronunciation Keys, p. 35.)

Accentuate the Syllable

Syllables are words or parts of words in which a vowel sound is heard. Syllables can be simple phonemes, or sounds that have no particular meaning. Syllables can also be morphemes, or sounds that have meaning. Accents tell which syllable in a word receives emphasis. For example:

banana = ba nan´a   **friendship =** friend´ ship

Sometimes more than one syllable is stressed. The louder syllable takes the *primary* accent. The less loud stressed syllable takes the *secondary accent*. For example:

elementary = el´ e men´ ta ry   **cafeteria =** caf´ e te´ ri a

Prefixes and Suffixes

Prefixes

Prefixes are groups of letters at the beginnings of words that have meaning. When a prefix is attached to a word, its meaning combines with the meaning of the original word to form a new word. *Prefix* is a good example. *Pre-* comes from Latin and means "before." *Fix* means "to attach." So *prefix* means "to attach before"—in this case, to attach before a word.

Common Greek and Latin Prefixes

Prefix	Origin	Meaning	Example
acro-	Greek	top, high	acrobat (walker up high)
aero-	Greek	air	aerobic (using air)
alti-	Latin	high	altitude (height)
amphi-	Greek	both, around	amphibian (living in both air and water)
ana-	Greek	not, wrong	anachronism (in the wrong time frame)
andro-	Greek	man	android (robot with human features)
ante-	Latin	before	antebellum (before the war, usually the Civil War)
anthro-	Greek	man	anthropology (study of humans)
aqua-, aque-	Latin	water	aquarium (water-filled tank)
arch(i)-	Greek	chief, main	architect (building designer)
archaeo-	Greek	very old	archaeology (study of human life in the past)
arthro-	Greek	joint	arthropod (animals, usually insects, with jointed legs)
astro-	Greek	star	asteroid (star that moves through space)
atmo-	Greek	vapor, gas	atmosphere (layer of gases surrounding a planet)
audio-	Latin	sound, hearing	audiometer (instrument used to test hearing)
baro-	Greek	weight	barometer (instrument that measures air pressure)

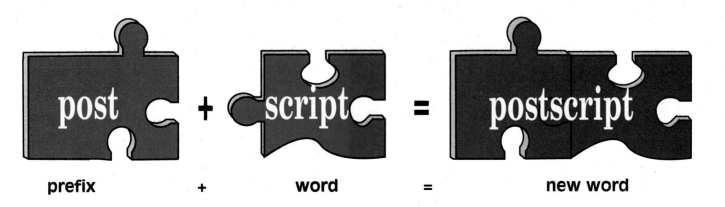

post + script = postscript

prefix + word = new word

Prefix	Origin	Meaning	Example
biblio-	Greek	book	bibliography (list of books)
bio-	Greek	life, living	biology (the science of living things)
centi-	Latin	hundred	centennial (100-year anniversary)
chloro-	Greek	green	chlorophyll (substance that makes plants green)
chrono-	Greek	time	chronology (list of events in the order in which they happened)
circum-	Latin	around	circumference (distance around a circle or sphere)
co-	Latin	together	cooperate (work together)
contra-	Latin	against	contradict (say the opposite)
cosmo-	Greek	universe	cosmic (having to do with the universe)
crypto-	Greek	hidden, secret	cryptogram (message written in code)
de-	Latin	not, put down	deny (say something is not true)
deca-	Greek	ten	decade (10 years)
deci-	Latin	tenth	decimal (based on the number 10)
denti-	Latin	tooth	dentist (tooth doctor)
di(s)-	Latin	apart	disconnect (take apart)
dia-	Greek	through	diameter (straight line that passes through the center of a circle)
digit-	Latin	finger	digits (the numbers 0 through 9; fingers and toes)
dino-	Greek	terrible	dinosaur (terrible lizard)
dyna-	Greek	force	dynamite (powerful explosive)
equi-	Latin	equal	equivalent (equal in amount, value, or meaning)
geo-	Greek	earth, land	geography (study of Earth's surface)
glosso-	Greek	tongue	glossary (list of words and their meanings)
grapho-	Greek	written, writing	graphology (study of handwriting)
helio-	Greek	sun	heliocentric (arrangement of planets with a sun in the center, as in our solar system)
hemi-	Greek	half	hemisphere (half of a sphere)
hetero-	Greek	different	heterogeneous (made up of different parts)
hexa-	Greek	six	hexagon (flat figure with six sides and six angles)
homo-	Greek	same	homophones (words that sound the same)
hydro-	Greek	water	hydroelectric (electricity coming from waterpower)
hypno-	Greek	sleep	hypnotize (to relax someone into a sleeplike condition)
il-, im-	Latin	not, against	illegal, imperfect (against the law; not perfect)
inter-	Latin	between	interplanetary (between planets)
intra-, intro-	Latin	inside	introduce (make known; bring inside)
iso-	Greek	equal	isosceles triangle (triangle with two equal sides)
magni-	Latin	great	magnificent (great in beauty, importance, or decoration)

Prefix	Origin	Meaning	Example
mal(e)-	Latin	evil, bad	malice (bad feeling, wanting to do evil things to others)
mega-	Greek	great	megaphone (cone-shaped tube that, when talked through, makes the human voice louder, or greater)
metro-	Greek	measure	meter (basic unit of measuring length in the metric system)
micro-	Greek	small	microscope (instrument that makes small things appear larger)
mono-	Greek	one	monotone (unchanging tone or pitch; drone)
multi-	Latin	many	multitude (many people or things)
neo-	Greek	new	neonatal (newborn)
nocti-	Latin	night	nocturnal (active at night)
ob-	Latin	against	object (go against)
octa-	Latin	eight	octagon (flat figure with eight sides and eight angles)
omni-	Latin	all	omnivore (animal that eats both plants and animals)
ped-, pedi-	Latin	foot	pedal (foot-operated lever)
pedo-, pedi-	Greek	child	pediatrician (doctor for babies and children)
per-	Latin	thorough, complete	perfect (complete in every way)
poly-	Greek	many	polygon (flat figure with many sides)
post-	Latin	after	postscript, p.s. (note added after the signature on a letter)
pre-	Latin	before	previous (event that happened before)
pro-	Latin	for	promote (work for the growth or success of a person, idea, company, etc.)
re-	Latin	again	return (come again)
retro-	Latin	backward	retrorocket (rocket fired in the opposite direction of a larger rocket to slow it down)
rhino-	Greek	nose	rhinoceros (large mammal with one or two large horns on its snout)
sub-	Latin	below, under	submerge (put under water)
super-, supra-	Latin	above	superior (in a position above)
terra-	Latin	land	terrarium (glass tank used to grow plants or raise small land animals)
trans-	Latin	over, across, beyond	transport (carry over land, water, or through air)
ultra-	Latin	beyond	ultrasonic (having to do with sounds that are beyond the ability of humans to hear)
uni-	Latin	one	unicorn (imaginary horselike animal with one horn growing from the top of its head)

Suffixes

Suffixes, like prefixes, combine their meanings with the meaning of the words to which they are added to form new words. But suffixes are "fixed," or attached, to the **ends** of words.

Many suffixes change the original word from one **part of speech** to another. For example, the suffix **-er** changes the verb **teach** to the noun **teacher**. The suffix **-er** also is used to make comparisons. My dog is **nice** but my cat is **nicer.** The suffix **-ing** is also used to change one part of speech to another, often a verb to a noun. For example, **teach** to **teaching** (see also Gerunds, p. 53). The suffix **-ing** is also used to form present participles (see p. 43). Another common suffix in English is **-ed**. It is used to form the past participles of regular verbs (see p. 43) and to form adjectives from nouns. For example, Robin Milligan has a strong will. The strong-willed student is Robin Milligan.

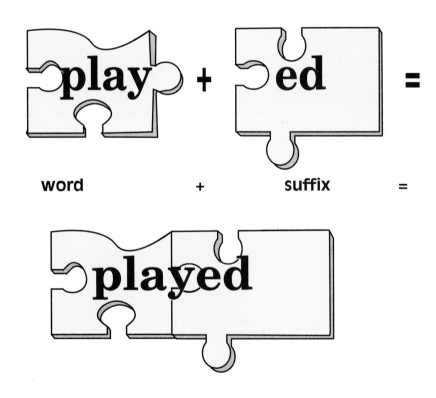

word   +   suffix   =

new word

Common Greek and Latin Suffixes

Suffix	Origin	Meaning	Example
-archy	Greek	rule	monarchy (state or country ruled by a king, queen, or emperor)
-biosis	Greek	life	symbiosis (two or more living things that support each other)
-chrome	Greek	color	monochrome (picture presented in one color only)
-cide	Latin	kill	homicide (murder)
-cracy	Greek	form of rule	democracy (government run by people, not by a king, queen, emperor, or dictator)
-derm	Greek	skin	epidermis (outer layer of skin)
-drome	Greek	running	hippodrome (arena for horse race or show)
-emia	Greek	of the blood	anemia (blood without enough red blood cells)
-fuge	Latin	away from	refuge (shelter or protection from danger)
-gamy	Greek	marriage	monogamy (marriage to one person at a time)
-geny	Greek	bearing	progeny (children)
-gon	Greek	angle	polygon (flat figure with four or more angles)
-grade	Latin	walking	centigrade (scale for measuring progressing temperature, progressing from freezing at 0° to boiling at 100°)
-gram, -graph	Greek	writing	telegraph (message sent by a device that uses electrical wires)
-hedron	Greek	having sides	polyhedron (solid figure with many sides)
-iatrics	Greek	treatment of disease	geriatrics (medical treatment of senior citizens)
-itis	Greek	disease	arthritis (joint disease)
-lepsy	Greek	attack	narcolepsy (sudden attack of sleepiness)
-lith	Greek	made of stone	monolith (large freestanding stone)
-logy	Greek	spoken, a theory or science	paleontology (science of prehistoric life)
-mania	Greek	type of madness	kleptomania (uncontrollable desire to steal)
-meter	Greek	instrument	thermometer (instrument used for measuring temperature)
-nomy	Greek	laws ruling	astronomy (science of outer space)
-oid	Greek	in the form of	asteroid (small bodies in space that orbit the sun)
-opia	Greek	of the eye	myopia (nearsightedness)
-ous	Latin	having the qualities of, full	beauteous (having the qualities of beauty)
-pathy	Greek	feeling, suffering	antipathy (strong feeling of dislike)
-phany	Greek	appearance	epiphany (sudden appearance of the solution to a problem, or the meaning of a phrase or sentence, etc.)
-phobia	Greek	fear, dread	claustrophobia (fear of being closed into small places)
-phone	Greek	sound	homophone (sounds that are the same but are spelled differently)

3 Spelling Sounds and Words

Five Basic Rules for Spelling

1 Words containing ie or ei
I before *e*, except after *c*, or when sounding like *a*, as in **neighbor** and **weigh**.
piece, deceive

Exceptions to the "i before e" rule include ceiling, conceit, either, foreign, height, leisure, neither, sheik, species, *and* weird.

2 Silent or final e
If a word ends with a silent *e*, drop the *e* before adding a suffix that begins with a vowel.
bore/boring love/loving skate/skating
Do *not* drop the silent *e* before adding a suffix that begins with a consonant.
bore/boredom hate/hateful skate/skateboard

3 Final y
If a word ends in a consonant followed by *y*, change the *y* to *i* before adding a suffix.
cry/cried friendly/friendliness gloomy/gloominess
If a word ends in *y* with a vowel before it, do not change *y* to *i* before adding suffixes or other endings.
destroy/destroyed play/playing volley/volleys

Exceptions to the "silent e" include argument, ninth, *and* truly.

4 Consonant preceded by a vowel
If a one-syllable word ends with one consonant with a vowel before it, double the final consonant before adding a suffix.
can/canned nut/nutty pot/pottery
If a multisyllable word ends with a consonant preceded by a vowel and the accent is on the last syllable, double the final consonant before adding a suffix.
acquit/acquittal control/controlling repel/repellent

If a suffix begins with i, do not change the y, for example: crying, dryish.

5 One-plus-one rule
When a prefix ends in the same letter with which the main word begins, include both of the repeated letters.
il- + logical = illogical mis- + spell = misspell
When a suffix begins with the same letter with which a main word ends, include both the repeated letters.
accidental + ly = accidentally mean + ness = meanness
The one-plus-one rule also applies to making compound words. Include all letters of both words, even if they are repeated.
room + mate = roommate

If a word with more than one syllable ends in a consonant preceded by a vowel but the last syllable is unaccented, do not double the consonant before adding a suffix, for example: travel/traveler, honor/honorable, *and* widen/widened.

Commonly Mispelled Words

accessory	congratulations	glacier	occurred
accompany	conscience	government	omitted
acquaintance	conscious	grammar	parallel
acquire	corduroy	guarantee	plaid
address	cough	guess	potatoes
all right	counterfeit	guest	prairie
a lot	debt	handkerchief	privilege
already	definite	height	probably
Antarctic	dependent	independence	raspberry
arithmetic	desperate	judgment	receipt
asthma	diarrhea	kindergarten	reference
athlete	disappear	laugh	relieve
available	dumb	league	rhythm
banana	eighth	library	ridiculous
bargain	environment	license	sandwich
beauty	exaggerate	literature	scissors
believe	exceed	maintenance	separately
broccoli	excel	mathematics	special
calendar	exercise	mattress	squirrel
cantaloupe	exist	misspell	tomatoes
caterpillar	fascinate	mosquitoes	truly
ceiling	February	necessary	Tuesday
cemetery	forehead	neighbor	usually
chief	formally	niece	vaccinate
cinnamon	formerly	noticeable	vacuum
committee	freight	nuisance	Wednesday
	gauge	obedience	

Homophones, Homonyms, and Homographs

Homophones are sounds that are the same but are spelled differently. For example, *f* and *ph* are often used to spell the same sound, as in:

fine or file and phone or physical

C and *s* can also spell the same sound, as in:

circus or cereal and symbol or sign

And *g* and *j* can also spell the same sound, as in:

refuge or sergeant and jump or jinx

The word *homophone* comes from the Greek words *homo* (same) and *phone* (sound). It is also used to describe *homonyms*, or words that sound the same but have different meanings. The word *homonym* also comes from Greek words, *homo* and *onyma* (name). (See also The Secret of Nyms, p. 34.)

Homonyms that not only sound the same but are also spelled the same are called homographs. *The word* homograph *comes from the Greek words* homo *and* graph, *which mean "same writing" (see Prefixes and Suffixes, pp. 19–23).*

Please mail this letter.	**We wore our swimsuits to the pool.**
The letter came in the mail.	**Mom drives to work in a car pool.**
The knight wore armor and chain mail.	**I have a pool table in my basement.**

Familiar Homonyms

allowed/aloud	I was ***allowed*** to play my stereo after school. We read ***aloud*** in class.
ant/aunt	The ***ant*** is a frequent visitor at picnics. My ***aunt*** is my father's sister.
ate/eight	I ***ate*** lunch at school last week. I have ***eight*** video games.
bare/bear	Don't walk outside in your ***bare*** feet. The ***bear*** lives in the woods.
berry/bury	The ***berry*** from that bush is poisonous. The squirrel tried to ***bury*** the acorn.
blew/blue	The storm ***blew*** in from the west. ***Blue*** is my favorite color.
brake/break	I had to ***brake*** to slow down my bicycle. I didn't mean to ***break*** the glass vase.
capital/capitol	Please remember where to use ***capital*** letters. We met Senator Smith in the ***capitol*** building.
cent/scent/sent	I don't have a ***cent*** to my name! That perfume has an awful ***scent***. I ***sent*** a letter to my best friend.
colonel/kernel	The ***colonel*** led the soldiers in battle. I found only one unpopped ***kernel*** in the popcorn bowl.
dear/deer	My puppy is very ***dear*** to me. I saw some ***deer*** at the petting zoo.
fair/fare	The weather is ***fair*** today. I paid full ***fare*** for my airplane ticket.
feat/feet	The acrobat performed a breathtaking ***feat*** on the high wire. My ***feet*** hurt from standing too long.
flew/flu/flue	The birds ***flew*** past my window. I had the ***flu*** over spring vacation. The smoke and ash rose up the chimney ***flue***.
flour/flower	We'll need some ***flour*** to make the pancake batter. The violet is our state ***flower***.
heal/heel/he'll	That scratch should ***heal*** quickly. My new shoes rubbed a blister on my ***heel***. ***He'll*** be coming round the mountain when he comes.

hear/here	Please speak louder because I can't **hear** you. Come over **here**!
heard/herd	I **heard** the news on the radio. A **herd** of cattle moves to the lower pasture every afternoon.
hole/whole	My dog dug a **hole** in the backyard. I read the **whole** book in one morning.
hour/our	I'll be ready in one **hour**. **Our** next meeting is in one month.
know/no	I didn't **know** half the answers on the quiz. **No**, I don't think I passed.
loan/lone	She asked him to **loan** her money for lunch. When the other frogs left, Ribbet was the **lone** frog in the pond.
mail/male	I put the letter in the **mail** yesterday. It was an all-**male** club and no girls could join.
main/mane	I think I understand the **main** idea of the story. That male lion has a thick, beautiful **mane**.
meat/meet	I'm vegetarian now, so I don't eat **meat**. **Meet** me at the mall at seven o'clock.
one/won	Give me **one** good reason for going to study hall. Our team **won** at the science fair.
pail/pale	I took my little sister's **pail** and shovel to the beach. Your face went **pale** when your name was called.
pain/pane	Cleaning my room is a real **pain**. The window was made of one large **pane** of glass.
pair/pear	I have one **pair** of jeans. The apple looks tastier than the **pear**.
peace/piece	The two countries signed a **peace** treaty. I had a **piece** of that delicious chocolate cake.
plain/plane	The skirt was **plain**, but the blouse was fancy. We flew on a **plane** to visit my grandfather.
pray/prey	Let's **pray** for good weather for our field trip. Eagles and owls are birds of **prey**.
principal/principle	The **principal** idea of the story is that people should get along. My teacher is a person of **principle**.
rain/reign/rein	The **rain** fell for two days before the sun came out again. The queen's **reign** won't end until she dies. She told me to take the horse by the **reins**.
right/write	Turn **right** at the corner. **Write** a letter to your uncle.
role/roll	I auditioned for a **role** in the school play. My favorite lunch is peanut butter and jelly on a **roll**.
sail/sale	The captain and crew set **sail** in their three-masted ship. My mother says I can't get the jacket until it's on **sale**.

scene/seen	She painted a forest *scene* in art class.
	I haven't *seen* her since three o'clock.
soar/sore	Did you see the eagle *soar* through the sky?
	Throwing the ball made the new pitcher's arm *sore*.
some/sum	Have *some* pie if you're hungry
	The *sum* of two and two is four.
son/sun	The father had one *son* and three daughters.
	The *sun* rises in the east.
stair/stare	It took the baby a long time to climb each *stair*.
	Looking around is fine, but please don't *stare*.
stationary/stationery	The statue is *stationary* so you can't move it.
	Use nice *stationery* for writing thank-you notes.
steal/steel	He used to *steal* pennies from his sister's piggy bank.
	The car body is made of *steel*.
suite/sweet	The *suite* of rooms was decorated in blue and green.
	The lemonade was too *sweet*.
tail/tale	My dog has a very long *tail*.
	Did you read the *tale* of Paul Bunyan and Babe, the blue ox?
their/there/they're	*Their* house is on the next block.
	Her dog is *there*, behind the fence.
	They're going to be happy after the quiz.
threw/through	She *threw* the ball past home plate.
	The ball flew *through* the air.
to/too/two	I went *to* the dance.
	My friend came, *too*.
	The *two* of us danced together.
waist/waste	I like my belt around my hips, not my *waist*.
	Don't *waste* that perfectly good paper.
wait/weight	Please *wait* for me.
	I'd guess your *weight* to be about 70 pounds.
way/weigh	Let's take the back *way* home.
	How many pounds do you *weigh*?
weak/week	She grew thin and *weak* from her illness.
	It took one *week* to recover.
wear/where	I thought I'd *wear* cutoffs to camp.
	Where did I put my homework?
weather/whether	The *weather* was warm and sunny.
	I don't know *whether* I should go or not.
which/witch	*Which* witch is *which*?
	The *witch* knew hundreds of spells.

Palindromes semordnilaP

mom

dad

noon

level

radar

Palindromes are words, phrases, and sentences that read the same way forward and backward!

Madam, I'm Adam.

Able was I ere I saw Elba.

A man. A plan. A canal: Panama.

Rats live on no evil star.

Abbreviations

Abbreviations are shortened forms of words. They are made by leaving letters out or by replacing a group of letters with another letter or symbol.

AC	alternating current (type of electrical current)	C.I.A.	Central Intelligence Agency
		cm	centimeter
A.D.	anno Domini (Latin for "in the year of the Lord," or since the birth of Christ)	C.O.D.	cash on delivery
		C.P.A.	certified public accountant
a.m.	ante meridiem (from midnight until noon)	C.P.R.	cardiopulmonary resuscitation
		D.A.	district attorney
asap	as soon as possible	DC	direct current (type of electrical current)
A.S.P.C.A.	American Society for the Prevention of Cruelty to Animals		
		D.C.	District of Columbia
B.A.	Bachelor of Arts (college degree)	D.D.S.	doctor of dental surgery
B.C.	before Christ	DNA	deoxyribonucleic acid (the basic material of genes)
B.C.E.	before the Christian era		
B.S.	Bachelor of Science	DOA	dead on arrival
C	centigrade or Celsius	ed.	editor, edition
c.	copyright or circa	ESP	extrasensory perception

esp.	especially		**MSG**	monosodium glutamate (flavor enhancer)
et al.	et alia (and others)		**NAACP**	National Association for the Advancement of Colored People
etc.	et cetera (and so forth)			
F	Fahrenheit (scale for measuring temperature)		**no.**	number
			oz.	ounce
F.B.I.	Federal Bureau of Investigation		**p.**	page
FYI	for your information		**p.m.**	post meridiem (from noon until midnight)
G.O.P.	Grand Old Party (Republican party)			
Hon.	the Honorable		**P.S.**	postscript
H.R.H.	His Royal Highness, Her Royal Highness		**pt.**	pint
			qt.	quart
i.e.	id est (that is)		**R.F.D.**	rural free delivery (U.S. mail category)
I.Q.	intelligence quotient		**R.I.P.**	rest in peace
I.R.S.	Internal Revenue Service		**R.N.**	registered nurse
K	1,000		**RR**	railroad
k.	karat (unit of weight)		**R.S.V.P.**	répondez s'il vous plaît (French for please respond)
kg	kilogram			
km	kilometer		**S.A.S.E.**	self-addressed, stamped envelope
l	liter		**St.**	street, saint
l.	latitude		**t.**	ton
lb.	*libra* (pound)		**TNT**	trinitrotoluene (an explosive)
M.D.	*medicinae doctor* (doctor of medicine)		**UFO**	unidentified flying object
			UHF	ultrahigh frequency (radio waves)
mfg.	manufacturing		**v. or vs.**	versus (against)
ml	milliliter		**VCR**	videocassette recorder
mm	millimeter		**VHF**	very high frequency (radio waves)
mph	miles per hour		**w**	watt (unit for measuring electrical power)
ms.	manuscript			

Contractions

A contraction is formed by putting together two words with certain letters left out. An *apostrophe* (') is used in place of the missing letters.

aren't	are not	**she'd**	she had/she would
can't	cannot	**she'll**	she will
couldn't	could not	**she's**	she is
could've	could have	**shouldn't**	should not
didn't	did not	**should've**	should have
doesn't	does not	**there'd**	there had/there would
don't	do not	**there'll**	there will
hadn't	had not	**there's**	there is
hasn't	has not	**they'll**	they will
haven't	have not	**they're**	they are
he'd	he had/he would	**'twas**	it was
he'll	he will	**wasn't**	was not
he's	he is	**we'll**	we will
I'm	I am	**we're**	we are
isn't	is not	**weren't**	were not
it'd	it had/it would	**what'd**	what had/what would
it'll	it will	**what's**	what is
it's	it is	**won't**	will not
let's	let us	**wouldn't**	would not
mightn't	might not	**would've**	would have
might've	might have	**you'll**	you will
mustn't	must not	**you're**	you are

Using the Dictionary

1 The Parts of a Dictionary

Guide Words usually appear in the outer corner of each page of a dictionary. the first guide word identifies the first **main entry** on the page. The second word identifies the last word on the page.

New letters break the dictionary into different sections, based on alphabetical order.

Main entry word or words are usually set in bold type.

Illustrations are used to add visual reinforcement to written definitions.

Pronunciation of the main entry follows the entry word or words.

rabbi ▶ radar

Rr

rab·bi (rab-eye) *noun* A Jewish religious leader.

rab·bit (rab-it) *noun* A small, long-eared, furry mammal that lives in a hole that it digs in the ground. *See* **angora** *picture*.

rab·ble (rab-uhl) *noun* A noisy crowd of people.

ra·bies (ray-beez) *noun* A fatal disease that makes dogs and other animals go mad. ▷ *adjective* **rabid** (rab-id)

rac·coon (ra-koon) *noun* A mammal with a ringed tail and black-and-white face markings that look like a mask.

race (rayss)
1 *noun* A test of speed. *To run a race.*
2 *noun* One of the major groups into which human beings can be divided. People of the same race share the same physical characteristics, such as skin color, which are passed on from generation to generation.
3 *verb* To run or move very fast.

race car

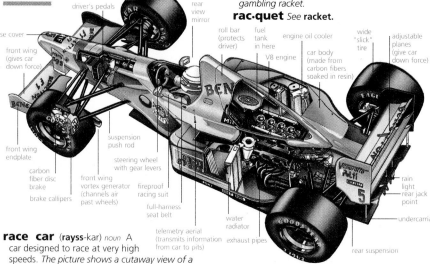

driver's pedals
rear view mirror
nose cover
front wing (gives car down force)
front wing endplate
carbon fiber disc brake
brake callipers
suspension push rod
steering wheel with gear levers
front wing vortex generator (channels air past wheels)
fireproof racing suit
full-harness seat belt
telemetry aerial (transmits information from car to pits)
roll bar (protects driver)
fuel tank in here
engine oil cooler
V8 engine
car body (made from carbon fibers soaked in resin)
exhaust pipes
water radiator
wide "slick" tire
adjustable planes (give car down force)
rain light
rear jack point
undercarriage
rear suspension

race car (rayss-kar) *noun* A car designed to race at very high speeds. *The picture shows a cutaway view of a Camel Benetton Ford B1938 Formula I race car.*

race re·la·tions (rayss ree-lay-shuns) *noun*
The way that people of different races get along when they live in the same community.

196

ra·cial (ray-shuhl) *adjective*
1 To do with a person's race. *Racial characteristics.*
2 Between different races. *Racial harmony.*

ra·cist (ray-sist) *noun* A racist is someone who thinks that some races are better than others or treats people unfairly or cruelly because of their race. ▷ *noun* **racism,** *adjective* **racist**

rack (rak)
1 *noun* A framework for holding things or for hanging things from. *A clothes rack.*
2 *noun* An instrument of torture used in the past to stretch the body of a victim.
3 *verb* If you **rack your brains** you think very hard. *I racked my brains to remember his name.* ▷ **racking, racked**

rack·et (rak-uht) *noun*
1 **racket** *or* **racquet** A stringed frame with a handle that you use in games such as tennis, squash, and badminton. *See* **badminton** *picture.*
2 A very loud noise.
3 A dishonest activity. *The police exposed a gambling racket.*

rac·quet *See* **racket.**

ra·dar (ray-dar) *noun*
1 Planes and ships use **radar** to find solid objects by reflecting radio waves off them. Radar is an acronym for RAdio Detecting And Ranging.

Variations in spelling follow the preferred spelling of the main entry.

Parts of speech are identified for each main entry or subentry.

Word divisions are shown in the main entry for words of two or more syllables.

Definitions of the main entry follow the listing of pronunciation and part of speech. Definitions tell the meaning of the main entry.

Multiple definitions are provided for words with more than one meaning.

radial ▶ rage

2 **radar trap** A system set up by the police to catch speeding drivers by using radar equipment.

ra·di·al (**ray**-dee-uhl) *adjective*
1 Spreading out from the center.
2 To do with a kind of automobile or truck tire whose design makes it tougher than a traditional tire.

ra·di·ant (**ray**-dee-uhnt) *adjective*
1 Bright and shining.
2 Someone who is **radiant** looks very healthy and happy.
▷ *noun* **radiance**, *adverb* **radiantly**

ra·di·ate (**ray**-dee-ate) *verb*
1 To spread out from the center.
2 To send out something strongly. *Mario radiates confidence.*
▷ *verb* **radiating, radiated**

ra·di·a·tion (**ray**-dee-**ay**-shun) *noun*
1 The sending out of rays of light, heat, etc.
2 Particles that are sent out from a radioactive substance.

ra·di·a·tor (**ray**-dee-ay-tur) *noun*
1 A metal container through which hot water or steam circulates, sending out heat into a room.
2 A metal device through which water circulates to cool a vehicle's engine. *See* **car, race car** *pictures.*

▶ Word History
The word **radical** comes from a Latin word that means "root" or "origin." Something that is radical affects even the roots of a problem or situation.

ra·di·cal (**rah**-duh-kuhl) *adjective*
1 If a change is **radical**, it is thorough and has important and far-reaching effects.
▷ *adverb* **radically**
2 Someone who is **radical** believes in extreme political change. ▷ *noun* **radical**

ra·di·o (**ray**-dee-oh)
1 *noun* A piece of equipment that you use to listen to sounds sent by electrical waves.
▷ *adjective* **radio**
2 *verb* To send a message using a radio.
▷ *verb* **radioing, radioed**

ra·di·o·ac·tive (**ray**-dee-oh-**ak**-tiv) *adjective*
If an object is **radioactive**, it gives off strong, usually harmful rays. ▷ *noun* **radioactivity**

ra·di·o·graph·y (**ray**-dee-og-ruh-fee) *noun*
The process of taking X-ray photographs of people's bones, organs, etc.
▷ *noun* **radiographer**

ra·dish (**rad**-ish) *noun* A small red and white vegetable that you eat in salads. *See* **vegetable** *picture.* ▷ *noun* **radishes**

ra·di·um (**ray**-dee-uhm) *noun* A radioactive element sometimes used to treat cancer.

ra·di·us (**ray**-dee-uhss) *noun*
1 A straight line drawn from the center of a circle to its outer edge. *See* **circle** *picture.*
2 The outer bone in your lower arm. *See* **skeleton** *picture.*
3 A circular area around a thing or a place. *Most of my friends live within a radius of a mile from my house.*
▷ *plural noun* **radii** (**ray**-dee-eye)

raf·fle (**raff**-uhl) *noun* A way of raising money by selling tickets and then giving prizes to people with winning tickets.
▷ *verb* **raffle**

raft (raft) *noun*
1 A floating platform, often made from logs tied together.
2 *verb* To travel by raft. ▷ *noun* **rafting**
3 *noun* An inflatable rubber craft with a flat bottom.
▷ *verb* **rafting, rafted**
The picture shows an inflatable raft traveling through fast-moving water.

inflatable rafting

rag (rag) *noun*
1 A piece of old cloth.
2 **rags** *noun plural* Very old, worn-out clothing.

rage (rayj)
1 *noun* Violent anger.
2 *verb* To be violent or noisy. *The wind raged around the house.* ▷ *verb* **raging, raged**

Some words that begin with an "r" sound are spelled "wr."

197

33

Dictionary Notations

Synonyms and Antonyms

synonyms: able/strong

Pearl is an *able* athlete and as *strong* as any member of the team.

antonyms: able/weak

She is an **able** student, although her eyes are so **weak** she must wear thick glasses.

synonyms: absent/elsewhere

The principal was *absent*, because she was needed *elsewhere*.

antonyms: absent/present

Marcia was *absent* today, but her brother was *present* for roll call.

synonyms: add/sum up

I'll *add* the list and then you *sum up* to double-check me.

antonyms: add/subtract

When you *add* the bill, please *subtract* the credit for the CDs I returned

Synonyms and Antonyms

What is the secret of **nym**? Well, the secret is revealed in **morphemics**, the study of the meanings of units of sound (see also p. 5).

First, consider **nym**. **Nym** comes from the Greek **onoma,** meaning "name."

Next, consider the Greek words **ant** and **syn**. **Ant** means opposite. **Syn** means "like" or "same."

Now, put **nym** together with the other words:

Ant + (o)nym = antonym   A word of opposite meaning

Syn + (o)nym = synonym   A word of similar or like meaning

You've now discovered the secret of nym!

Pronunciation Keys

Vowels

a *or* ă	p<u>a</u>t
ä *or* ah	f<u>a</u>ther
ā *or* ay *or* a◡e	s<u>ay</u>, p<u>ai</u>d, f<u>a</u>te
â(r)	<u>air</u>, d<u>are</u>
ar	b<u>ar</u>n
aw *or* ô	r<u>aw</u>, b<u>a</u>ll
e *or* ĕ	m<u>e</u>n
ē *or* ee	s<u>ee</u>m
ēr *or* ihr	f<u>ear</u>
i *or* ĭ	s<u>i</u>t
ī *or* eye	<u>i</u>con (eye-kon), r<u>ye</u>, t<u>i</u>re
o *or* ŏ	h<u>o</u>t
ō *or* oh	t<u>oe</u>, t<u>o</u>te
ô *or* or	m<u>o</u>re
oi	<u>oi</u>l
ŏŏ	b<u>oo</u>k
ōō	<u>oo</u>ze
ou	<u>ou</u>t
oor	p<u>oor</u>
ou	<u>ou</u>t, n<u>ow</u>
u *or* ŭ	p<u>u</u>t
û(r) *or* ur	b<u>ur</u>n
uh	r<u>u</u>nt, comm<u>a</u>
ə *or* uh	<u>a</u>lone, r<u>e</u>buke, eas<u>i</u>ly, scall<u>o</u>p, min<u>u</u>s

Consonants

b	<u>b</u>in, ca<u>b</u>in, ca<u>b</u>
ch	<u>ch</u>ild
d	<u>d</u>o, gla<u>dd</u>en, ba<u>d</u>
f	<u>f</u>oe
g	<u>g</u>o
h	<u>h</u>am, be<u>h</u>ave
j	<u>j</u>et, re<u>j</u>ect, fu<u>dg</u>e
k	<u>k</u>ic<u>k</u>, <u>c</u>all
l *or* ll	<u>l</u>et, wi<u>ll</u>, marshma<u>ll</u>ow bund<u>l</u>e
m	<u>m</u>an, su<u>mm</u>er, hi<u>m</u>
n	<u>n</u>o, ba<u>nn</u>er, o<u>n</u>
p	<u>p</u>in, su<u>p</u>er, si<u>p</u>
r	<u>r</u>un, flu<u>rr</u>y, stee<u>r</u>
s *or* ss	<u>s</u>it, mi<u>ss</u>es, pa<u>ss</u>, pa<u>c</u>e
sh	<u>sh</u>ow, fa<u>sh</u>ion, ba<u>sh</u>
t	<u>t</u>en, bu<u>tt</u>on, sen<u>t</u>
th *or* TH	<u>th</u>in, e<u>th</u>er, wi<u>th</u> / <u>th</u>is, wi<u>th</u>er
v	<u>v</u>an, ri<u>v</u>er, ro<u>v</u>e
w	<u>w</u>ill, a<u>w</u>ay
wh	<u>wh</u>ale, <u>wh</u>ich, no<u>wh</u>ere
y	<u>y</u>es, on<u>i</u>on
z	<u>z</u>oom, la<u>z</u>y, tho<u>s</u>e
zh	mea<u>s</u>ure, mira<u>g</u>e

Acronyms

Acronyms are words formed from the first letters or syllables of words in phrases or titles. They are related to *abbreviations* (see p. 29–30), the shortened versions of words or phrases. *Acronyms* don't end with periods, and are usually written in all capital letters.

AIDS	acquired immune deficiency syndrome (disease)
BASIC	Beginner's All-purpose Symbolic Instruction Code (computer language)
CARE	Citizens for American Relief Everywhere (a relief organization)
CAT scan	computerized axial tomography (medical test)
DOS	disk operating system (computer operation program)
EPCOT	Experimental Prototype Community of Tomorrow
FICA	Federal Insurance Contributions Act (Social Security)
GATT	General Agreement on Tariffs and Trade
LASER	light amplification by stimulated emission of radiation
loran	long-range aid to navigation (navigation tool)
MADD	Mothers Against Drunk Driving (organization to prevent drunk driving accidents)
NASA	National Aeronautics and Space Administration (U.S. space agency)
NATO	North Atlantic Treaty Organization (peacekeeping agency)
NOW	National Organization for Women
OPEC	Organization of Petroleum Exporting Countries
PIN	Personal Identification Number (used for bank cards, credit cards, etc.)
radar	radio detecting and ranging (navigation device)
RAM	random-access memory (short-term computer memory)
ROM	read-only memory (built-in computer memory)
SADD	Students Against Drunk Driving (organization to prevent drunk driving accidents)
UNICEF	United Nations International Children's Emergency Fund (relief organization)
VISTA	Volunteers in Service to America (helping organization)
WHO	World Health Organization
ZIP code	zone improvement plan (post office delivery code)

PARTS OF SPEECH

1 Nouns

Nouns are words that name people, places, or things. Nouns come in many forms.

Common and Proper Nouns

Common nouns are general names for people, places, and things:

backpack, friend, holiday, mall, school, teacher, video

Proper nouns are names for specific people, places, and things. Proper nouns always begin with a capital letter.

E. T.   Mrs. Johnson
Jackson School   Nintendo®
Jenny   Oakdale
Labor Day   Saturday

Concrete and Abstract Nouns

Concrete nouns name people, places, and things that you can see, touch, taste, hear, or smell.

fire, library, music, perfume, pizza, snow, woman

Abstract nouns name ideas, feelings, or qualities.

beauty, democracy, fairness, health, kindness, love, sadness

Three Little Words: Articles

Three little words—*a*, *an*, and *the*—mark the presence of nouns. These words are called *articles*. Articles are either *definite* or *indefinite*. The definite article, *the*, refers to specific or known things. The indefinite articles, *a* and *an*, refer to unspecific nouns. For example, if you are about to go on a trip, your mom will tell you to get into *the* car. Of course she means your family's car. If your older sister wants a big 16th birthday present, she might ask your parents for *a* car. This means any car, as long as it's hers.

Collective Nouns

Collective nouns name groups of people, places, or things.

class, club, committee, humankind, orchestra

Compound Nouns

Compound nouns are made up of two or more words. Compound nouns can be **common**, **proper**, **singular**, **plural**, **concrete**, **abstract**, or **collective**. They can be one word, two words, or hyphenated.

baseball, daydreams, electric guitar, jack-o'-lantern

Singular and Plural Nouns

Singular nouns name only one person, place, or thing. *Plural* nouns name more than one person, place, or thing.

MAKING A SINGULAR NOUN PLURAL

1. Add an *-s* to the end of most singular nouns to make them plural.

   dog + s = dogs   cat + s = cats   test + s = tests

2. Add *-es* to the end of a singular noun ending in **ch**, **s**, **sch**, **sh**, **x**, or **z** to make it plural.

   dress + es = dresses   lunch + es = lunches   quiz + es = quizzes

3. Change *f* to *v* and add *-es* to the end of most singular nouns ending in *f*, *lf* or *fe* to make them plural. There are exceptions to this rule!

   knife/knives   leaf/leaves   life/lives

   exceptions: sniff/sniffs   safe/safes

4. Drop the *y* and add *-ies* to a singular noun ending in a consonant followed by *y* to make it plural.

   fly/flies   battery/batteries   penny/pennies

5. Add an *-s* to a singular noun ending in a vowel followed by *y* to make it plural.

   day/days   key/keys   boy/boys

6. Add *-es* to most words ending in *o* preceded by a consonant to make them plural.

   potato/potatoes   echo/echoes   tomato/tomatoes

7. Add an *-s* after the most important word in a hyphenated compound noun or to one written as two words to make it plural.

   brother-in-law/brothers-in-law   computer drive/computer drives

8. Memorize odd plurals.

   man/men   woman/women   goose/geese   foot/feet

2 Pronouns

Pronouns are words that can be substituted for nouns in naming people, places, and things.

Personal and Possessive Pronouns

Personal pronouns refer to people or animals.

I, you, he, she, it, we, they, me, him, her, us, them

They told us that they were going to meet her at the mall.

Sometimes personal pronouns are used to show possession or ownership. These personal pronouns are sometimes called *possessive pronouns.*

my, mine, your(s), his, her(s), its, our(s), their(s), whose

If this bubble gum isn't hers, then it must be mine.

 Never use an apostrophe in a possessive pronoun!

Presto, Change-o:

Substituting Pronouns for Nouns

Subject Pronouns

Subject pronouns are often used with a noun or another pronoun as part of the subject of a clause or sentence (see pp. 54–57).

These and those are very different.

She and I went to the movies last Saturday.

Some had a great time at the party. Others did not.

Object Pronouns

Object or *predicate pronouns* are often used with a noun or another pronoun as part of the direct object (see Subjects and Predicates, p. 54).

Fred saw him at the fair.

We share the dog. It belongs to her and me.

Always speak of yourself last.

Demonstrative Pronouns

Demonstrative pronouns refer to specific people, places, or things.

this, that, these, those

Which ice skates are lighter, these or those?

Indefinite Pronouns

Indefinite pronouns refer to or replace nouns in a general way. Some indefinite pronouns are also used as adjectives. They are then followed by a noun, as in *both cats* or *each flower*. Examples follow:

all, any, anyone, both, each, either, every, many, neither, nobody, no one, nothing, other(s), several, some, someone

Anyone can try out for the team, but only some will make it.

Reflexive Pronouns

Reflexive pronouns are used to refer back to subject nouns and pronouns.

myself, yourself, himself, herself, itself, ourselves, yourselves, themselves

Cathy knew she could do it herself.

Intensive Pronouns

Intensive pronouns are reflexive pronouns that emphasize a noun or another pronoun.

John himself, she herself, the team themselves

We ourselves formed the new reading club.

Interrogative Pronouns

Interrogative pronouns are pronouns used to ask questions.

what, which, who, whom, whose

What is happening and to whom?

3 Verbs

Verbs are words that describe action or a state of being.

Action and Linking Verbs

Action verbs describe activity. Action can be physical.

eat, leap, read, run, sleep, swim, walk, yell

Abe Lincoln walked seven miles to school every day.

Action can also mean quieter activities.

care, concentrate, forgive, grow, hate, love, think

A tree grows in Brooklyn.

Linking verbs do not describe action, but a state of being. They connect a noun or adjective to the subject of a clause or sentence.

Jose was happy.

The plan looks good.

HELPING VERBS

Helping verbs help the main verb describe action that happened in the past, is happening in the present, or will happen in the future. There are 23 helping verbs.

am	being	do	have	must	were
are	can	does	is	shall	will
be	could	had	may	should	would
been	did	has	might	was	

A main verb can have up to three helping verbs.

The bus is coming at three o'clock.

Oops! The bus must have gone at 2:55.

We could have gone on the bus if you hadn't forgotten your backpack in your locker.

Infinitive Form

An *infinitive* is a main verb usually preceded by the word *to*. It does the work of both a verb and a noun, and it may be used as an adjective or adverb.

noun →

To go often is her goal.   verb

I like to play the piano.

A desire to study often brings success in school.

adjective

Verb Tenses

The *tense* of a verb tells you the time the action takes place or the state of being — past, present, or future. There are six main tenses:

1 **Present tense. The present tense means** now.
The dog *has* fleas.
I *go* to school every day.

2 **Past tense. The past tense means** before **now.**
The dog *had* fleas until he had a flea shampoo.
I *went* to school last week.

3 **Future tense. The future tense means** not yet.
The dog *will have* fleas if he sleeps in the barn.
I *will go* to school next Monday.

4 **Present perfect tense. The present perfect tense means** started in the past and continuing up to the present.
The dog *has had* fleas for three years.
I *have gone* to school on the bus for years.

5 **Past perfect tense. The past perfect tense means** finished before some other past action.
The dog *had had* fleas for two years before he stopped scratching.
I *had gone* to fourth grade before I started fifth grade.

6 **Future perfect tense. The future perfect tense means** action will start and finish in the future.
Two months after they are born, the vet *will have given* all the puppies a flea collar.
I *will have gone* to school for three months before we get a break.

Participles

A *participle* is a form of a verb that can be used as a verb or as an adjective. There are two kinds of participles—present and past.

Present participles usually end in -ing and follow the helping verbs for to be (see p. 41).

Jeff is going to be George Washington in the school pageant.

Amy will be playing Martha Washington.

Past participles usually end in -ed or -en, or -d, -t, or -n, and follow the helping verbs have or had.

Rowan had decided to try out for band instead of the pageant.

Marty and Courtney have been chosen for the parts of John and Abigail Adams.

Principal Parts of Verbs

Each verb has three main parts, called *principal parts*. The principal parts include:

1. The infinitive

to swim, to run, to throw

2. The past tense

swam, ran, threw

3. The present participle

(to be) swimming, (to be) running, (to be) throwing,

4. The past participle

(have/had) swum, (have/has) run, (have/had) thrown

Regular and Irregular Verbs

Regular verbs are verbs that can be changed from the present to the past and past participle simply by adding *-ed* or *-d*.

Now I jump. Yesterday I jumped. I have jumped.

Now we skate. Yesterday we skated. I have skated.

The past tense and past participles of irregular verbs are formed in unpredictable ways.

You do what you like. I did my homework, and Ian has done his.

To Be or Not to Be

The verb *to be* is the most often used verb in the English language. It is an irregular verb. In fact, there are eight different words in the verb to be.

is, am, are, was, were, be, being, been

Now I am. Yesterday I was. I have been.

Now we are. Yesterday we were. We have been.

Just being here is great!

4 Adjectives

Adjectives are words that describe nouns and pronouns. Adjectives *modify*, or tell more about, nouns. They answer one of three questions:

1 What kind?
Eric watched the magnificent eagle soar through the sky.

2 How many?
Katie checked out eight books from the library.

3 Which one(s)?
Ben took that route to the farm.

Common Adjectives

Common adjectives describe nouns in a general way. These adjectives tell just about anything, from size, shape, and number to color, design, and character.

big, friendly, green, round, spotted, twelve

The big dog growled at me.

The friendly dog doesn't growl.

Twelve dogs can make a lot of noise.

Proper Adjectives

Proper adjectives are formed from proper nouns. They are always capitalized.

America/American, Asia/Asian, Queen Victoria/Victorian

I love American music.

We have Asian students from China, Japan, and Thailand.

That Victorian house looks haunted.

Demonstrative Adjectives

Demonstrative adjectives are the same words as demonstrative pronouns (see p. 40).
As adjectives, they go with nouns and answer the question "Which one(s)?".

that, these, this, those

That movie was great, but those songs were awful.

This candy tastes good, but these peanuts are rotten.

USING ADJECTIVES TO COMPARE

Comparisons can be made on three levels, or **degrees** — positive, comparative, and superlative.

1 **The positive degree describes one thing.**
Kyle was *good* at solving riddles.
Kyle is *short*.

2 **The comparative degree compares two things.**
Kyle's sister was *better* than he.
Kyle's sister is *shorter*.

3 **The superlative degree compares three or more things.**
Kyle's brother was the *best* riddle solver of all.
Kyle's brother is *shortest*.

To compare adjectives (and adverbs, see p. 47):

1 **Add -er and -est to most adjectives that are one or two syllables long.**
big/bigger/biggest   strong/stronger/strongest

2 **If the one- or two-syllable adjective ends in y, drop the y and add -ier and -iest.**
happy/happier/happiest   homely/homelier/homeliest   silly/sillier/silliest

3 **Use more and most or less and least in front of most adjectives with two or more syllables.**
advanced/more advanced/most advanced   capable/more capable/most capable

4 **Add -r and -st to short adjectives that end in e.**
little/littler/littlest   subtle/subtler/subtlest   able/abler/ablest

5 **Some adjectives are irregular and don't follow these rules, for example:**
bad/worse/worst   good/better/best

5 Adverbs

Adverbs describe a verb, adjective, or another adverb. Adverbs are used to make meaning clearer or more exact.

Adverbs and Verbs

Adverbs answer four questions about the verbs they describe — how, when, where, and to what extent?

The young girl jumped high. **She danced** beautifully.

The tall boy came late. **He apologized** immediately.

The dog barked loudly **when he was** here. **The child sat** there.

The elderly man swam daily. **He enjoyed it** thoroughly.

Adverbs and Adjectives

Adverbs usually answer the question "How?" when they describe adjectives.

The very young girl danced beautifully.

The extremely tall boy came late.

The annoyingly noisy dog barked loudly.

The exceptionally elderly man swam daily.

The extremely tall boy came very late.

Adverbs and Adverbs

Adverbs answer the questions "How?" or "How much?" when they describe other adverbs.

The young girl jumped exceptionally **high.**

The tall boy came very **late.**

The noisy dog barked really **loudly.**

The elderly man swam amazingly **fast.**

Comparing Adverbs

Adverbs can be compared, just like adjectives, by using the positive, comparative, and superlative degrees (see p. 45).

**I run fast enough to make the track team, but
Amy runs faster, and Tamika runs fastest.**

A WHOLE NEW WORD:

Making Adverbs from Adjectives

Many adjectives can be changed into adverbs by adding *-ly* to the end.

loud/loudly, quick/quickly, bad/badly

But this magic doesn't apply to the three most common adverbs in the English language: *not*, *very*, and *too*.

LOUD LY

6 Prepositions

Prepositions relate a noun or pronoun to another word in the same sentence. A preposition can also connect a pronoun to a noun in a sentence. A preposition usually tells where something is, where something is going, or when something is happening. A preposition always introduces a phrase. The noun at the end of the prepositional phrase is the *object of the preposition* (see also p. 52).

The cups are over **the sink.**

Lee went to the concert with **Kim.**

Mary ran to **her mother.**

The cat ran after **the mouse.**

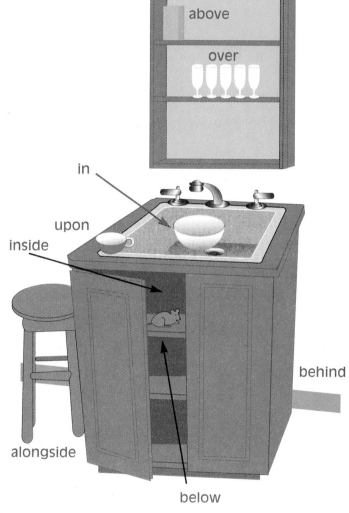

List of Common One-, Two-, and Three-Word Prepositions

about	but	off
above	by	on
according to	despite	on account of
across	down	onto
after	due to	out
against	during	out of
ahead of	except	outside
along	except for	over
along with	for	past
among	from	since
around	in	through
as	in addition to	throughout
as for	in back of	to
as to	in case of	toward
at	in front of	under
away from	in regard to	underneath
because of	inside	until
before	in spite of	up
behind	instead of	upon
below	into	up to
beside	like	with
between	near	within
beyond	of	without

(See also Prepositional Phrases, p. 52.)

7 Conjunctions

Conjunctions are words that join words, phrases, clauses, and sentences.

Coordinating Conjunctions

Coordinating conjunctions join words, phrases, and sentences.

and, but, nor, so, or, yet

The kids came late and baked a cake.

I went to the ballpark but the game was canceled.

I have a sled yet it never snows here.

I can neither eat nor drink before I play soccer.

Subordinating Conjunctions

Subordinating conjunctions join dependent clauses to independent clauses.

after, although, as, as if, because, before, for, if,
once, since, so, so that, than, that, though, till,
unless, until, when, whenever, where, whereas, wherever,
whether, while

Father came home after the work was done.

We were happy once the ice cream was served.

Daniel practiced his music so that he could try out for band.

I cannot go until she comes.

Correlative Conjunctions

Correlative conjunctions are always used in pairs in a phrase or sentence even though they are split up by other words.

both/and, either/or, neither/nor, not only/but also, whether/or

The hungry elephant ate not only the pretzels but also the peanuts.

You should have given him either the pretzels or the peanuts.

Yes, but he wanted to have both the pretzels and the peanuts.

Adverbial Conjunctions

Adverbial conjunctions join clauses or sentences of equal importance.

accordingly, besides, consequently, furthermore, hence, however, likewise, moreover, nevertheless, so, still, therefore, thus

The pretzel bag was left open; consequently, the pretzels went stale.

My dog doesn't like peanuts; however, he loves peanut butter!

I think, therefore I am.

8 Interjections

Interjections are words, phrases, and nonsense words that express strong feelings. Interjections are *interjected* into, or interrupt, a smooth flow of thoughts to emphasize certain feelings, for example, excitement, happiness, sadness, fear, or anger. Interjections stand apart from sentences and are usually punctuated with exclamation points (see p. 60).

aha, ahem, alas, all right, eureka, gracious, hello, help, hey, oh, oops, ouch, phew, thanks, ugh, well, wow, yikes, yippee, yuck

Aha! I've caught you!

Oops! You put the coin in the wrong slot.

Yuck! What a mess!

9 Phrases, Clauses, and Sentences

Some words convey powerful emotion or action just by themselves.

But most words need to be combined with other words to get your message across.

Phrases

Phrases are any groups of two or more words that together form a thought or express one meaning. A phrase has no subject or verb. There are four basic types of phrases: prepositional, participial, infinitive and gerund, and verb phrases.

Prepositional Phrases

Prepositional phrases are groups of two or more words that begin with a preposition and end with a noun or pronoun. The noun or pronoun is known as the *object of the preposition*.

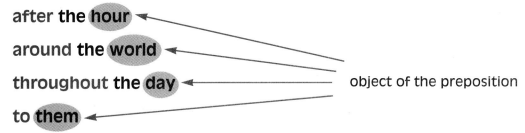

after **the hour**

around **the world**

throughout **the day**   object of the preposition

to **them**

A pronoun immediately following a preposition is always the object of the preposition.

after **her**

by **us**

without **them**

Participial Phrases

Participial phrases are groups of two or more words that begin with *participles* (see p. 43).

writing **a book**

grasping **his sword**

leaping **to my feet**

Infinitive and Gerund Phrases

Infinitive phrases are groups of two or more words consisting of an infinitive verb or an infinitive verb plus an adverb. Infinitive verbs are easily identified. They begin with the word *to*.

to go

to go boldly

to play

to care deeply

Gerund phrases are groups of two or more words that contain a gerund. A gerund is a verb form that ends in *-ing* and acts as a noun.

my being there

his going to the moon

your wanting a new skateboard

APPOSITIVES

Appositives follow the nouns, pronouns, or phrases in clauses that they describe. Appositives can be one word or a whole phrase. Appositives are separated from a main clause or sentence with commas.

Boston, Massachusetts, is north of Providence, Rhode Island.

Freddy, Sue Ellen's dog, howled.

Verb Phrases

Verb phrases are groups of two or more verbs that describe an action. They are made up of a main verb and one or more helping verbs.

have come

had gone

will be coming

would have come

should be going

(See also Participles, p. 43.)

Clauses

Clauses are groups of two or more words that have a *subject* and a *predicate*. Clauses are either *principal* or *subordinate*.

Principal Clauses

Principal clauses are also called *independent*, or *main, clauses*. Only principal clauses can stand alone as complete *sentences* (see pp. 55–57).

The dog was sick.

The dog ate grass, and the cat licked her paws.

Subordinate Clauses

Subordinate clauses are also called *dependent clauses*. Subordinate clauses express ideas or information related to principal clauses.

The dog was sick because he ate grass.

The cat licked her paws after she played with the yarn.

 Subordinate clauses cannot stand alone as sentences. They are combined with principal clauses to complete thoughts or give greater meaning to a sentence.

SUBJECTS AND PREDICATES:
Simple, Complete, and Compound

A *simple subject* is the noun or pronoun that tells who or what a clause or sentence is about.

The boy played soccer.

A *complete subject* is the noun plus any descriptive word or phrase that goes with it.

The athletic boy on the football field played soccer.

A *compound subject* is two or more simple subjects joined by a conjuction (see p. 49).

My mother and I watched the boy play soccer.

A *simple predicate* is just the verb in the predicate.

The horse whinnied.

A *complete predicate* is the verb plus any descriptive words or phrases that make up the predicate. It is everything in a clause or sentence that is not contained in the complete subject.

The horse whinnied loudly at the trainer.

A *compound predicate* is found in sentences where two or more different actions are described.

The horse whinnied and snorted.

Sentences

Sentences are groups of words that express a complete thought. You can make a sentence by putting a noun (subject) and a verb (predicate) together.

Sentences can be short or long, simple or complicated. But all sentences fall into one of three categories: simple, compound, or complex.

Noun (subject)	Verb (predicate)
I	go.
He	runs.
Mosquitoes	bite.
People	care.

Simple Sentences

A *simple sentence* is made up of one **subject** and one predicate.

The boys played **baseball.**

The boys played **baseball against the girls' team.**

The boys from Middletown played **against the Hightown girls' team.**

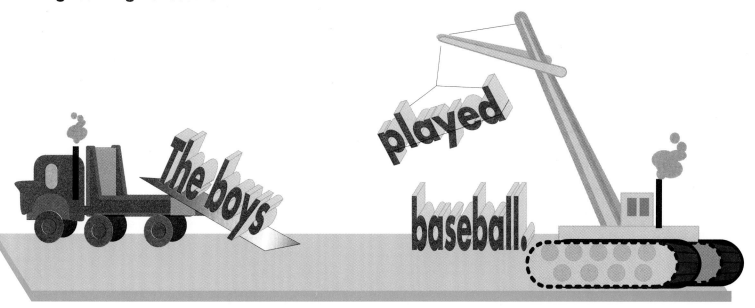

Compound Sentences

A *compound sentence* is made up of two or more simple sentences joined by a conjunction (see pp. 49–50).

The girls played baseball and they beat the other team.

I go to the playground with my brother every day, but yesterday he wouldn't play with me.

I like broccoli raw yet I can't eat it cooked.

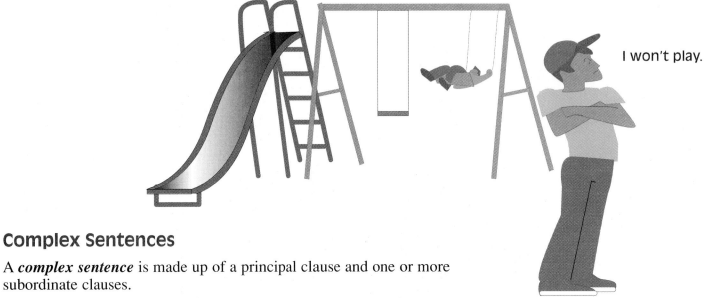

I won't play.

Complex Sentences

A *complex sentence* is made up of a principal clause and one or more subordinate clauses.

Fighting infection was difficult until penicillin was discovered.

When I forgot my lunch, I had to eat that gross cafeteria food.

The fifth graders left the playground early because it started to rain.

Four Types of Sentences

Declarative Sentences

Declarative sentences make statements.

Life is good.

I am happy, and you are sad.

You ate an extra scoop of ice cream.

Interrogative Sentences

Interrogative sentences ask questions.

Is life good?

Are you happy, too?

Did your stomach hurt after you ate the fifth scoop of ice cream?

Imperative Sentences

Imperative sentences give commands or request action.

Go.

Open the door, and go inside.

After you open the door, go inside.

You Understood

Imperative sentences often don't have subjects—or do they? When you give a command, you are addressing someone else. He or she knows whom you're talking to. The you is the subject, and whether or not you say it, *you* is understood.

(You) **Leave my cat alone.**

(You) **Go.**

Exclamatory Sentences

Exclamatory sentences express strong feelings or emotions. They end in exclamation points (see p. 60) instead of periods.

I feel horrible!

I ate a whole pizza and I'm still hungry!

I studied hard, so I got the highest score on the test!

PUNCTUATION MARKS and Some of Their Uses

Apostrophe (')

1. Shows possession

Jamai's shoe, the girls' toys, Mary's and John's boats

2. Shows contractions

can't, she's, would've, '98

3. Creates plurals of letters and symbols

3's, B's, 20's

Colon (:)

1. Introduces lists

The clock has three parts: a face, a dial, and numbers.

2. Introduces excerpts and long quotations

As Lincoln wrote in his Gettysburg Address: "Fourscore and seven years ago, our fathers brought forth on this continent a new nation, conceived in liberty and dedicated to the proposition that all men are created equal."

3. Separates hours from minutes when writing time in numerals

2:00, 4:15, 8:55

4. Punctuates the greeting in a formal letter

Dear Ms. President:

Comma (,)

1. Separates clauses in sentences, including long compound sentences.

The rain came, which was very good for the crops.

2. Separates items in a series

I want a baseball, a glove, and a bat for my birthday.

3. Separates three or more adjectives in a series

I saw red, green, yellow, and orange kites.

4. Separates a direct quotation in a sentence

Marty said, "Get out of there!"

5. **Separates a city from a state**

   Minneapolis, Minnesota

6. **Separates the month and day from the year in a date**

   June 6, 1994

7. **Sets apart mild interjections from the rest of a sentence**

   Gosh, I was hungry.

8. **Sets apart appositives**

   Bill, my brother, was late.

9. **Punctuates the greeting and closing in a friendly letter**

   Dear Sally,
   Your friend,

Dash (—)

1. **Works like a comma to separate phrases or clauses in a sentence**

   President Clinton — along with many others —
   studied law before entering politics.

2. **Works like a colon to separate lists**

   I had three choices — stand, run, or sit.

3. **Works like an ellipsis to show interrupted or unfinished statements**

   I would never have guessed, but then —

4. **Works like a comma to separate appositives**

   My father — a great guy — built a boxcar for the derby.

Ellipsis (. . .)

1. **Replaces words left out in the middle of a quote or obvious text**

   I pledge allegiance to . . . America.

2. **Shows that a thought or list should continue in the same pattern**

   A is for apple, b is for box, c is for cow . . .

3. **A period, followed by three ellipsis points shows that words have been left out at the end of a sentence, paragraph, or longer piece of writing.**

   I pledge allegiance to the flag. . . .

Exclamation point (!)

1. **Ends exclamatory sentences**
   I won!

2. **Separates an interjection from a sentence**
   Hooray! I won!

3. **Ends strong imperative sentences**
   Get away from the fire!

Hyphen (-)

1. **Connects two-part words**
   roly-poly, twenty-two, air-conditioning

2. **Separates words into syllables**
   ap-ple

3. **Connects compound nouns and adjectives**
   well-known man, teacher-in-training

4. **Separates some prefixes**
   ex-champion, re-create

5. **Divides words at the end of a line of writing**
   diction-   nota-
   ary   tion

Parentheses ( )

1. **Hold additional information in a sentence, but information that is not necessary to include in the sentence**
   I'll tell you (and you can listen to) my story.
   The girl was born (two weeks early) in Florida.

2. **Hold explanatory information or alternative spellings, names, or symbols**
   The gorgon (a mythical monster) frightened the sailors.
   The price was stated at fifteen dollars ($15).

Period (.)

1. Ends a declarative sentence

I will go to the zoo today.

2. Follows most initials

John F. Kennedy was a popular president.

3. Follows most abbreviations

The giraffe was 12 ft. tall.

4. Follows numerals when writing lists

1. Trading Cards
2. Bubble Gum, etc.
3. Milk

Question mark (?)

1. Ends an interrogative sentence

What are you doing up there?

2. Shows doubt or uncertainty when written in parentheses

King Tut lived 3,000 (?) years ago.

Quotation marks (" ")

1. Show a person's exact words

The teacher said, "Start writing."

2. Set apart titles of articles in magazines and newspapers

Did you read the story "Amazing Facts" in Sunday's paper?

3. Set apart chapter titles in books as well as essay, short story, song, and poem titles

"Getting Started" was the title of the first chapter of *Building a Treehouse*.

4. Set apart special words and phrases, including slang, non-standard English, and technical words

The answer to the clue "fruity" was the word "apple."
She had totally "radical" high tops.

5. When single (' / '), show a quotation within another quotation

"The teacher said, 'You kids are too much,' when we locked the classroom door," Fred explained to the principal.

Semicolon (;)

1. Joins related independent clauses into one sentence when they are not joined by a conjunction

The Great Houdini died; he could not make his greatest escape.

2. Sets apart items in a list, particularly items following a colon

This is what we need to do for the party: send the invitations; bake the cake; buy the candles, paper plates, napkins, and forks; and reserve the party room.

Underline (＿＿＿)

1. Sets apart book, movie, play, opera, TV show, and video titles

Have you read <u>Little House on the Prairie</u>?

2. Sets apart the names of newspapers and magazines

I read the article in <u>Junior Scholastic</u>.

3. Sets apart foreign words and phrases

<u>Adiós</u>, my good friends.

4. Adds emphasis to words and phrases

She told us <u>never</u> to eat with our hands.
He mentioned <u>a long time ago</u> that he would be going.

Note: In typeset books or on a word processor, italic type (*or italics*) is used in place of underlining. Italic type looks a little like cursive handwriting. In this book's typeface, *italic type looks like this.*

Sentence Diagrams

Life is good.

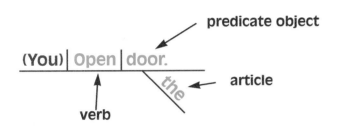

You ate an extra scoop of ice cream.

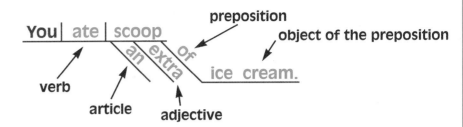

Open the door.

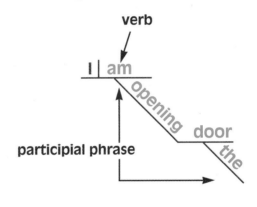

I am opening the door.

Yes, the hungry elephant ate not only pretzels but also peanuts.

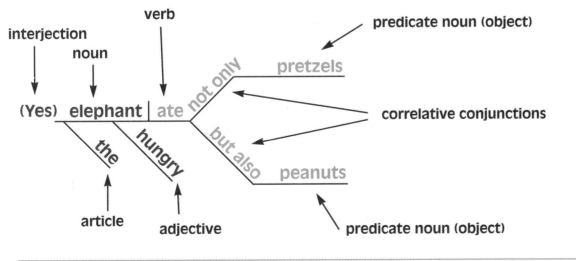

■ **Subject**

■ Predicate

10 Combining Sentences to Make Paragraphs

Paragraphs are groups of sentences that describe the same idea. A good paragraph includes the following: a topic sentence, detail sentences, proper order, and a consistent theme.

Topic Sentences

The *topic sentence* states the theme or main idea of a paragraph. It is usually the first sentence of a paragraph, but it can also be found at the end. A topic sentence is almost never found in the middle of a paragraph.

Detail Sentences

Detail sentences tell more about the main idea of the paragraph.

Order of Sentences

The *order of sentences* is important in writing good paragraphs. For example, if you wrote a paragraph explaining the four steps in flossing your teeth, you wouldn't start by writing, "Throw the used dental floss away." Order should always make sense.

Theme

The *theme*, or main idea, holds all the sentences in a paragraph together. It is stated in the topic sentence. Be sure all the detail sentences stick to the theme and tell about the main idea. Sentences that do not belong upset the sense or flow in the order of the sentences. The sentences that don't make sense are called non sequiturs, or ideas that "don't follow."

Topic Sentence. Remember, the topic sentence states the *theme* of the paragraph. It is usually the first sentence.

Growing orange plants is as easy as one-two-three. First save the seeds from the next orange you eat. Next, place the seeds about one inch apart on top of a container filled with potting soil. Fast, cover with about a quarter inch of additional potting soil, water, and wait. If you keep your container in a sunny place and make sure the soil stays moist, your orange seeds should sprout in two to three weeks.

Detail Sentences. In this paragraph, they tell more about growing orange plants.

Order of Sentences. In order to make sense, the detail sentences must follow a logical order or *sequence*. Imagine rewriting the paragraph starting with the third sentence. It would make no sense.

WRITING TOOLS

1 Outlines and Story Maps

Outlines: Skeletons for Organized Writers

Outlines are tools that are used in the planning stages of writing, sometimes called *prewriting.* Outlines help you organize ideas for a school report or a speech. If you have a hard time getting all your ideas into an outline, it may mean you have chosen too large a topic. For example, it you are reporting on a trip to the zoo, you might find it easier to write about one of the exhibits or one zoo activity rather than try to describe every exhibit that you visited or every animal that you saw. A story on big cats or feeding time will allow you to say a lot on one interesting subject.

▶ *Outlines include three basic elements: a title, main headings, and subheadings. Together these elements help you create logical beginnings, middles, and endings for your work. Outlines also help you decide where it makes sense to include the information you want.*

Bats

I. The body
  A. Wings
    1. Only mammal that can fly
      a. They fly more slowly than most birds
      b. They can fly through tiny gaps and holes

Title
The *title* should tell the subject of the work. The title of the outline may or may not become the title of the paper.

2. The wings contract and fold along the bones when bats aren't flying

B. Head and Body
1. Strange face, sometimes really scary or ugly looking
2. Huge ears
3. Legs, but no arms-only wings
4. Sleep upside down

C. Senses
1. Almost blind
2. Echolocation
    a. Produce high-pitched sound
    b. Sound works like radar to help bat locate food or obstacles

Main Headings
Main headings state the main topics covered in the paper. The first is the opening paragraph, and the last is the conclusion. You can include as few as two other main headings or as many as you need to cover your subject. To show main headings, use a capital Roman numeral and a period.

II. Eating Habits
A. Most eat insects
B. Mice or other bats
C. Flower nectar
D. Fruit

Subheadings
Subheadings come under main headings. For the first level of subheadings, use capital letters. For the second level of subheadings, use Arabic numerals.

III. Life Cycle and Habitat
A. Live up to 20 years
B. Live birth, usually one baby at a time
C. Live almost anywhere in the world
1. Not in extremely cold places
2. Not on some islands
D. Some species migrate to find food
E. Species in cold climates hibernate in winter

Story Maps: The Path of Fiction

Story maps or *plans* are outlines for fiction writers. You can "map" the main parts of stories or plays: setting, characters, major events, problems (challenges), and solutions.

Story maps can be laid out in many different ways. Unlike outlines, you don't have to give the map a title or use Roman numerals. But, to be useful, the maps should include all the main parts of the story or play. These main parts should be organized around a **plot** (see p. 79), or action line.

Story Map

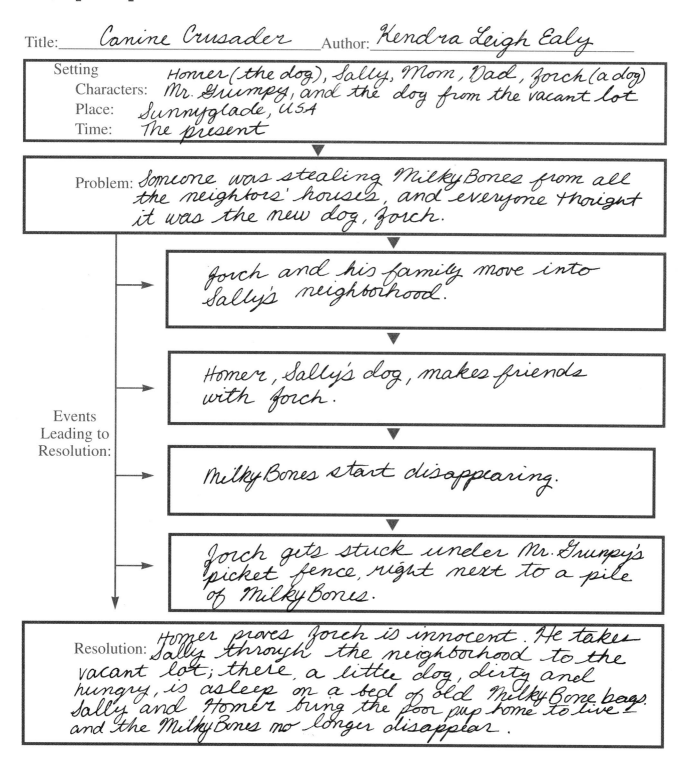

Title: *Canine Crusader*   Author: *Kendra Leigh Ealy*

Setting
Characters: *Homer (the dog), Sally, Mom, Dad, Zorch (a dog) Mr. Grumpy, and the dog from the vacant lot*
Place: *Sunnyglade, USA*
Time: *The present*

Problem: *Someone was stealing Milky Bones from all the neighbors' houses, and everyone thought it was the new dog, Zorch.*

Events Leading to Resolution:

Zorch and his family move into Sally's neighborhood.

Homer, Sally's dog, makes friends with Zorch.

Milky Bones start disappearing.

Zorch gets stuck under Mr. Grumpy's picket fence, right next to a pile of Milky Bones.

Resolution: *Homer proves Zorch is innocent. He takes Sally through the neighborhood to the vacant lot; there, a little dog, dirty and hungry, is asleep on a bed of old Milky Bone bags. Sally and Homer bring the poor pup home to live, and the Milky Bones no longer disappear.*

Venn Diagram

Use Venn diagrams to compare two or more characters or events.

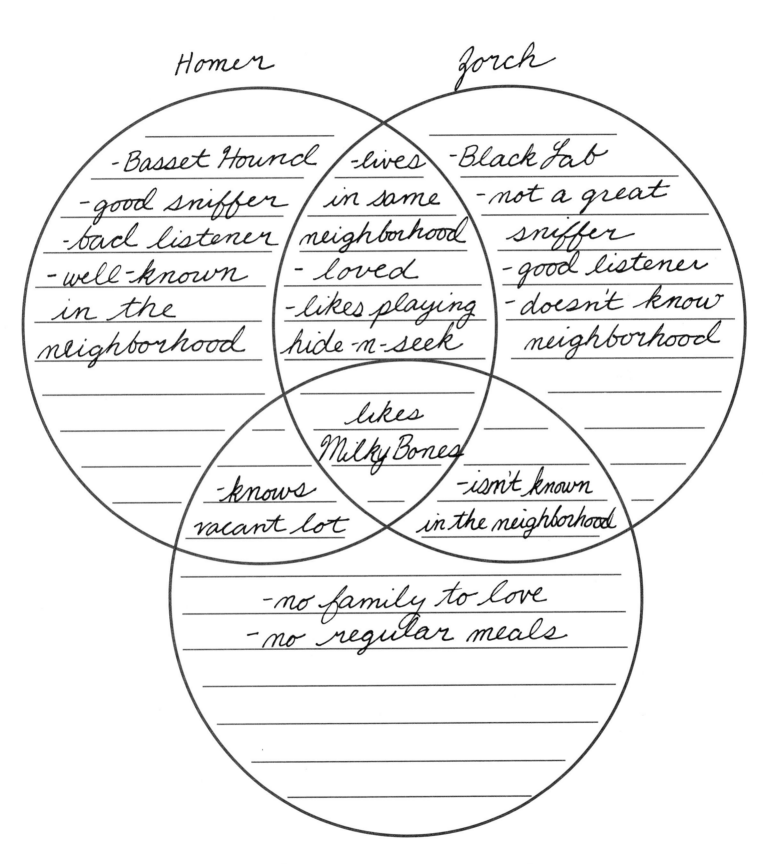

Homer

Zorch

- Basset Hound
- good sniffer
- bad listener
- well-known in the neighborhood

- lives in same neighborhood
- loved
- likes playing hide-n-seek

- Black Lab
- not a great sniffer
- good listener
- doesn't know neighborhood

likes Milky Bones

- knows vacant lot

- isn't known in the neighborhood

- no family to love
- no regular meals

Dog from Vacant Lot

2 Rough Draft to Final Copy

Once you've prepared an outline or a story map, you're ready to write the **rough** or **first draft**. The rough draft is also called **sloppy copy**.

Rough drafts help you organize your ideas into sentences. They also help show how the different parts of your writing fit together.

The rough draft is **not** the final copy. You may write several drafts before the final one. Don't worry about style and catchy phrases at this point. Instead, follow these basic steps:

1 Read over your outline, notes, or story map.

2 Follow your outline or map to write down in sentences the main points of the story.

 Skip a space between lines when you write your rough draft. Then you'll have plenty of room to make corrections or additions later.

3 Write down all your thoughts without stopping to check spelling or grammar, or to edit. Put in as much appropriate information as you can.

4 Read over your rough draft for obvious mistakes. Change sentences and paragraphs that do not follow logically. Mark corrections in grammar and punctuation (see next page).

5 Read over the rough draft for style. Consider how you might use some basic tools and techniques (see Terms and Techniques in Writing, pp. 76–80) to add drama or interest to your writing. Fill in details in your paper, or add minor characters, dialogue, or extra episodes to your fiction.

6 Put the rough draft aside for a while and then read it over again. Is there anything you want to rewrite? Would you like to show it to a friend or family member? Have you made your points clear? Try reading your work aloud to see if it sounds right. Fine-tune your copy.

7 Prepare a final draft.

Every Author Needs an Editor:
Editing Sense and Symbols

symbol	meaning	example
ℓ	delete	I went to the park ~~on Monday.~~ ℓ
∧	left out, insert	I went to the park ∧*yesterday*
∿	reverse order of letters (transpose)	I went to the park yes(t)(e)rday.
⊂	close up, no space	I went to the park ~~on Monday.~~
≡	write in capitals	I went to the park on m̲o̲n̲d̲a̲y̲.
. . . .	stet (let it stand)	I went to the park ~~on Monday.~~
¶	start new paragraph	I went to the park on Monday. Everyone was there, except Mary. She was home with the mumps. ¶Eric brought a soccer ball.
⊙	insert period	I went to the park ∧ I played on the swings.
∧	insert comma	I went to the park, ate candy ∧ and played.
ˇ	insert quotation marks	I said, ˇWait for me!ˇ
ˇ	insert apostrophe	The parkˇs benches are green.

75

3 Terms and Techniques in Writing

Alliteration

Repetition of the same sound at the beginning of two or more words that are next to each other or near each other.

Fly away, my fine-feathered friend.

Drat! I'd deem that a dastardly deed, Duane!

A silvery sliver slid from the needle case.

Allusion

Something or someone talked about through hints. *Allusions* are often made to people, places, and things that are already well known.

The poor dog died this afternoon. Now he is off to the big kennel in the sky. (Big kennel in the sky is heaven.)

He's no George Washington. (George Washington means honest person.)

Assonance

Vowel rhyme, or words that have the same vowel sound. *Assonance* is often used in poetry.

The slowly growing mighty oak did shade our home for years.

Cacophony

Noise, or harsh, unpleasant combinations of sounds. *Cacophony* is used in poetry for special effects. It is created by reading onomatopoeic words (see p. 79), or by adding sounds based on the author's instructions, for example, clapping hands, whistling, striking a triangle, etc.

Characters

The personalities in a story. Most *characters* are people, but sometimes characters are pets, wild animals, or fantasy creatures. The most important character in a book, story, play, or poem is called the *main character*. Other characters are called *secondary*, or *supporting, characters.*

In true stories, characters are drawn from real life. The main character in a biography is the person about whom the story is written. The secondary characters are people who have known or have somehow been involved with the life of the main character.

In fictional stories, characters are often good or bad, friendly or mean.

The "good" main character is called the *protagonist* and the "bad" main character is called the *antagonist*. A story can have many antagonists, but usually only one protagonist.

Many fictional characters suffer from a weakness called a *character flaw*. This flaw is important to the action or plot of the story (see Achilles' heel, p. 110) because it is the reason the character gets in trouble or falls into danger.

Climax

The high point of a story. It is followed by an ending called a resolution, or denouement.

Composition

Any written work, either fiction or nonfiction.

Dialogue

Conversation or talking that takes place between two or more characters. Dialogue is usually enclosed in quotation marks.

Figure of Speech

A word or phrase used to describe something in an imaginative and usually unrelated way. (See also *allusion, imagery, metaphor,* and *simile*.)

Hyperbole

A deliberate exaggeration used as a figure of speech.

My dog is as big as a ten-ton elephant!

Their house was so big, you had to drive a car from the front door to the living room.

My dog is as big as a ten-ton elephant.

Imagery

Word painting, or creating imaginary pictures with words. *Imagery* helps readers form pictures in their minds. These pictures make certain points easier to understand and more interesting to read. Such techniques as **allusion, metaphor**, and **simile** are examples of imagery.

My dog is very happy (without imagery).

My dog is a pig in mud (allusion).

The boy would not sit down at his desk (without imagery).

The boy's desk might well have been made of pins and needles (metaphor).

The yellow house was located on the top of a grassy hill (without imagery).

The house seemed to bloom atop the hill like a daffodil in April (simile).

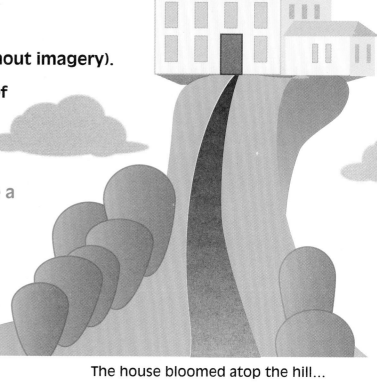

The house bloomed atop the hill...

Metaphor

A comparison of two different things to show a likeness between them that does not use *like* or *as*.

The teacher chimed the roll call.

Alice was drowning in tears.

Meter

The rhythm made by stressed and unstressed syllables in poetry.

There was a crooked man who walked a crooked mile . . .

There once was a penguin named Dave . . .

Mood

The feeling of a story, short story, poem, or play. Moods can be happy, sad, scary, tense, gloomy, etc.

Nonfiction

A piece of writing that tells about people, places, or events that exist, that are happening, or that have existed or happened in the past. Nonfiction can also express an opinion or true feeling.

Onomatopoeia

Words that are invented to imitate real sounds. **Bang, zip, smash, rip,** and **grrrrrr** are all examples of onomatopoeia.

Parable

A story with a moral or religious lesson to be learned. Parables are related to **fables**.

Personification

Attributing to things that are not human the personalities and actions of humans. Through personification, Pooh and Paddington behave like human children, not like bear cubs. Feelings can also be personified; for example, **fear grabbed** the victim in its **icy clutches**.

Plot

The actions or events in a short story, novel, or play.

Poetry

A feeling or story told in rhythmic verse. Poetry sometimes uses **rhyme** and **imagery**. A work of poetry is called a **poem**. (See also Writing Poetry, p. 86, and Poem Types and Terms, p. 87.)

Prose

Any writing that is like ordinary speech, unlike poetry.

Rhyme

The repetition of similar or identical sounds, for example:

red	green
bed	bean

Setting

The time and place in which a story, poem, or play takes place. A setting can be a forest, a house, a city, the present, the past, the future, etc.

Simile

A figure of speech that compares two unlike things. Similes are often confused with *metaphors*. A major difference between similes and metaphors is that a simile is introduced by the words *like* or *as*, and a metaphor is not.

The lion purred like a kitten.

Kim cried as if it were the end of the world.

Purrrrrrrrr

Subject

The *theme, topic*, or main idea of a sentence, paragraph, or larger piece of writing.

Theme

The main idea or *topic* in a piece of writing.

Tone

The feeling in a piece of writing, similar to mood. Tone or tone of voice reflects the feeling of the writer as much as the feeling in the writing. Tone can be nasty, kind, persuasive, angry, friendly, etc.

Topic

The main idea in a piece of writing

4 Understanding Other People's Writing

The tools you use to help you write—outlines and story maps—can also be used to help you understand other people's writing. So, too, can Venn diagrams, circle story frameworks, flow charts, time lines, and cause/effect diagrams.

Look at the following story about bats. It's broken down into outline pieces. Compare the pieces to the outline for this story (see pp. 66–67).

> ## Bats
> ## by K.C. Keneally
>
> Wings make bats one-of-a-kind among mammals. They are the only ones that have wings and can fly. Although bats fly more slowly than most birds, they are able to go through much smaller gaps and holes than our feathered friends. When bats aren't flying, they fold their wings along the wing bones and the flesh connects.
>
> Wings aren't the only things that make bats special. They have strange faces that are sometimes really ugly or even scary to look at.
>
> Most bats also have huge ears. They have legs, but no arms. Instead of arms, they have wings.

. Bat Bodies

A. Wings

B. Head and Body

C. Senses

Bats are mostly blind. Maybe you've heard the expression "blind as a bat"? Instead of seeing with their eyes, bats use echolocation. They send out a high-pitched sound that bounces off food and obstacles like radar. The bounced back sounds are picked up by receptors near the bat's ears.

Bats also sleep upside down.

II. Eating Habits

Most bats eat insects. Some eat mice or even other bats. Still other bats prefer flower nectar or fruits.

II. Life Cycle and Habitat

Bats can live up to 20 years. They are born live, like other mammals, and usually one at a time.

Except for remote islands and extremely cold places, bats are found everywhere in the world. Some bats survive happily in one place all year round. Others have to migrate to find food. In colder climates, bats hibernate during winter months when food is scarce.

Now look at the short story below. See how it can be broken down into the elements of a story map.

Characters
Place

Canine Crusaders
by *Kendra Leigh Ealy*

"Homer, fetch!" Sally Smith called to her dog. She tossed a Milky Bone toward the backyard fence of her home in Sunnyglade.

The bassett hound ran down the porch step and across the lawn. Then he raised his snout, positioned himself, caught the Milky Bone in his mouth, and plopped down on the spot to enjoy the tasty treat. Just then, a furry black streak flew over the fence and across the grass toward Homer.

"Zorch! Zorch, leave Homer alone!" Sally called after the streak. "I've got a treat for you, too!"

Zorch belonged to the Jeffersons. He and his family had just moved in next door. Zorch and Homer made friends on the spot.

Zorch couldn't have had a better friend than Homer. Everyone around Elm Street—everyone except Mr. Grumpy, of course—loved the sweet-tempered bassett and his constant companion, Sally. So everyone kept a bone or two on hand for their favorite dog. Zorch was quick to understand that Homer was top dog on Elm Street and, by association, he'd be popular, too!

Zorch was hounding Homer less than a week when the mystery of the Milky Bones began. The whole neighborhood was buzzing with the news. No sooner did Sally jump off the school bus than she heard all about it. Everybody's Milky Bones were missing!

Sally ran home, "Mom, where are the bones? Do you know the story? All the dog bones in the neighborhood are gone! Mom, did you hear?"

"Sally, Sally. Calm down," her mother said. "Yes, I've heard the news—but not before our Milky Bones were missing, too."

"Where'd they go, Mom?"

Homer bounded into the kitchen to greet Sally. He was about to leap to her waist and give her a lick, but she didn't open her arms for the greeting. Instead, he cocked his head to listen.

"Well dear, if we knew where the bones were, there wouldn't be a mystery," her mother replied. "The neighbors seem to think Zorch is the culprit, though."

"That's not fair!" Sally cried. "Zorch wouldn't do that!"

"Maybe not, dear, but that's what folks are saying," her mother said.

Sally and Homer moped out the back door and into the yard. No sooner had they hit the lawn than a black streak came flying over the fence.

"Not now, Zorch," Sally scolded. "This is no time for games—and no time for bones, either. You didn't steal the bones, did you, boy?"

Zorch sat near Sally's feet and cocked his head quizzically.

"Of course you didn't, Zorch," Sally answered her own question. "But we've gotta solve this mystery and get you off the hook."

Sally and the dogs walked around the house to Elm Street and turned along Spruce. "Am I imagining it," thought Sally, "or are people giving Zorch dirty looks?" The uncertain feeling grew stronger as she walked with the dogs over to Chestnut and around the corner onto Maple.

Just then, Homer picked up a scent. His hound dog instincts kicked in as he pressed his nose to the ground and slowly inched foward, following the trail of some mysterious odor. Homer was picking up speed, fast on the trail of something—on a canine crusade, Sally thought. Sally and Zorch followed Homer to the end of the block toward Mr. Grumpy's.

"Homer! Stay out of old man Grumpy's yard," she called. Mr. Grumpy was the only neighbor who never had a Milky Bone—or a kind word—for Homer.

But Homer followed the scent right into Mr. Grumpy's yard. Then, suddenly, Zorch bolted toward Mr. Grumpy's, too. Before Sally could stop them, the dogs ran out of sight toward mean Mr. Grumpy's backyard.

By the time Sally reached Grumpy's backyard, Homer was nowhere to be seen. Zorch was stuck under the backyard fence and barking his head off, and old man Grumpy was shouting from his back door.

"Get those vermin dogs outta my yard. I'll call the pound, I'm telling ya! Get those mutts outta here now!" Grumpy's threats were likely to become promises, Sally knew. She had to get Zorch unstuck and find Homer.

Sally knelt by Zorch and stroked his back. Zorch turned his head and gazed at her from the other side of the wire fencing. He took a deep breath and relaxed his muscles. Sally thought he would pull himself back into Grumpy's yard, but Zorch eased himself forward instead. He got clear of the fence and tore off behind Grumpy's toward the vacant lot. Sally chased after him and then Sally stopped, panting. She looked across the vacant lot. It was a great place for hide-n-seek, especially behind all the old tires and junk stashed there. But Sally didn't want to play hide-n-seek now—and she couldn't see Homer or Zorch anywhere.

"Homer, Zorch, come!" Sally hoped the dogs would answer her call. Sure enough, a black lab head popped up from behind an old bedspring in the middle of the lot. Then Homer came bounding into sight. He ran to Sally and took her pant leg in his mouth.

"Homer, stop it," Sally said. "Hey, no nipping."

Homer kept at it, tugging Sally's pant leg and pulling her toward the bedsprings.

"Okay, okay, boy," Sally said. "Are you trying to show me something?"

Sally followed Homer over to the far side of the bedsprings. There among the junk sat Zorch, feasting on Milky Bones—hundreds and hundreds of Milky Bones! But Zorch was not alone. With him was a scruffy dog with a filthy coat and no collar.

"Who are you, little fella?" Sally asked. "Whose doggy are you?"

The scruffy little dog sat back on his haunches and began to growl. But Zorch and Homer must have made some dog signal and their new friend backed off.

"Oh, I get it!" Sally exclaimed. "You're the Milky Bone thief and the Canine Crusaders have sniffed you out!"

"Don't worry, little guy. I'm not interested in your bones," Sally continued. "Now let's go home and tell the neighbors that the case of the missing Milky Bones is solved."

Sally, the crusaders, and Guy (as Sally came to name the scruffy little dog from the vacant lot) went home, steering clear of Mr. Grumpy's house, and frolicking all the way. Sally's dad went over to the lot after dinner with a wheelbarrow. He retrieved the stash of bones Guy had collected and redistributed them among the neighbors. Everyone laughed when they heard the story of the canine crusaders, and everyone came to love the new dogs in the neighborhood—just as much as, but not more than, Homer.

CREATIVE WRITING

1 Writing Poetry

Forms of Poetry

Poems come in many forms. Some rhyme, some don't. Some are long, some short. Some are funny, some are sad. But all poetry has a special rhythm and form that sets it apart from prose or ordinary speech. Two of the most popular poem forms among students are **haiku** and **limerick**.

Haiku

A poem written in three lines. The first line is five syllables long, the second seven syllables long, and the last five syllables long. Most haiku is about nature.

The white herons flew

Over the vast blue ocean

They fly there no more

Limerick

A humorous poem written in five lines. The rhyme scheme is a a b b a. The first, second, and last lines each have three strong beats. The third and fourth lines each have two strong beats.

A <u>pleasant</u> young <u>teacher</u> from <u>school</u>,	(a)
Not in<u>clined</u> to <u>playing</u> the <u>fool</u>,	(a)
Tripped <u>on</u> an er<u>aser</u>,	(b)
And <u>fell</u> without <u>grace</u>, "Er"	(b)
She <u>said</u>, that young <u>teacher</u> from <u>school</u>.	(a)

Poem Types and Terms

Ballad
A *narrative poem* that tells a story, often a sad one. Ballads, or ballades, have a tricky rhyme scheme. A literary ballad has three eight-line stanzas plus a quatrain at the end.

Blank verse
A poem in which the verses have a regular rhythm but do not rhyme.

Cinquain
A five-line stanza.

Couplet
A pair of lines that share something, usually rhythm and rhyme.

Elegy
A sad poem, most often written in honor of a dead person.

Epic
A long poem that tells a story, usually based on historic fact, about a hero and his actions. Homer's *Odyssey* is an example.

Lyric poem
A short, musical poem that expresses a feeling rather than tells a whole story.

Narrative poem
A poem that tells a story. It can be short or long.

Ode
A poem, often set to music, that has a theme of nobility or goodness.

Quatrain
A four-line stanza.

Sonnet
A love poem with a set rhyme scheme, written in 14 lines. Shakespeare wrote many sonnets.

Stanza
The paragraph of poetry. A stanza can be two lines long (as in a *couplet*), three lines long (as in a *haiku*), four lines long (as in a *quatrain*), five lines long (as in a *limerick*), or even fourteen lines long (as in a *sonnet*). The lines of a stanza share a set pattern, often a set meter, length, and rhyme scheme.

THE FIRST POETS

No one knows for sure who wrote the first poem. But we do know that ancient holy and wise people called shamans and druids created chants. The chants were rhythmic strings of words used as prayers and spells. Today, chants still stir strong emotions.

Shamans and druids were very powerful people in their societies. They were treated almost as kings and queens. Druids in the Celtic culture were also the keepers of history. Young druids went to school for seven years, learning — by memory — the history of their people from older druids. The history was chanted in verse to help the storyteller remember the story and to keep listeners entertained. In later years, these druids became known as *bards*. A bard is a singer or reciter of poetry.

Rhyme Schemes

Rhyme schemes are the patterns of rhyming words in poems. Rhyme schemes are written with small letters, beginning with *a*.

Couplet

When at last the sun is set	(a)
The fishers will haul in their net.	(a)

ABAB

When at last the sun is set	(a)
And the moon is risen above	(b)
The fishers will haul in their net	(a)
And peace will fly in with the dove.	(b)

AABB

When at last the sun is set	(a)
And the fishers have hauled in their net	(a)
The moon will rise above	(b)
And peace will fly in with the dove.	(b)

Writing a Poem

1 Choose a topic for your poem.

2 Choose a form of poetry or create a rhyme scheme and the rhythm. Read over a few of your favorite poems to get started.

3 Form a picture in your mind to help you express your feelings colorfully and briefly. Write down a few similes or metaphors you may want to use in your poem.

4 Write a rough draft of your poem. Concentrate on expressing your ideas. You can fix the rhyme scheme and rhythm later.

5 Check the rhythm and, if necessary, the rhyme scheme. Then rewrite or revise, if necessary.

(See also Rough Draft to Final Copy, p. 74.)

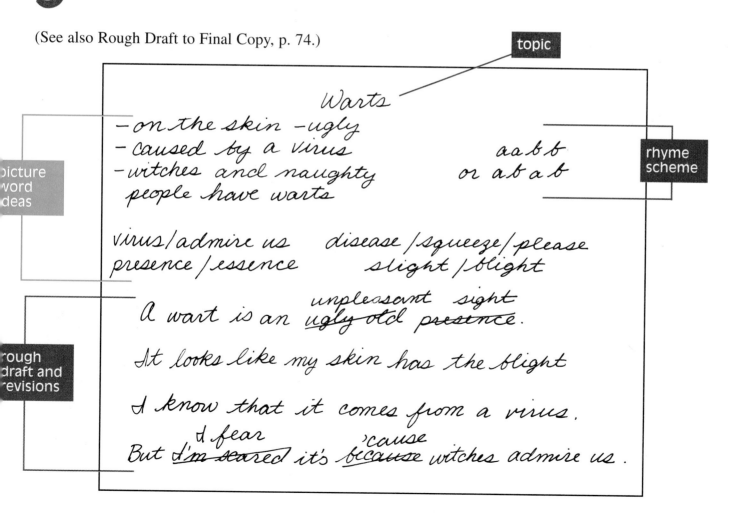

topic

Warts

picture word ideas
— on the skin — ugly
— caused by a virus
— witches and naughty people have warts

rhyme scheme
a a b b
or a b a b

virus / admire us   disease / squeeze / please
presence / essence   slight / blight

rough draft and revisions

            unpleasant sight
A wart is an ~~ugly old~~ presence.

It looks like my skin has the blight

I know that it comes from a virus.
      I fear   'cause
But ~~I'm scared~~ it's ~~because~~ witches admire us.

2 Writing Prose Stories

Prose Story Forms

Prose stories come in two basic forms: novels and short stories. *Novels* are long stories, with distinct beginnings, middles, and ends. Novels are usually divided into several chapters, and they have characters, setting, and plot. Many novels use dialogue to allow characters to talk to each other. Prose stories are also called *fiction*, something that is made up. Some writers create fiction entirely from their imaginations. Other writers create fiction based on real events or people.

Short stories also have beginnings, middles, and ends. They use characters, plot, and setting (see also Story Maps, p. 68).

Writing a Story

1 Choose the kind of story you want to write: for example, a mystery, true adventure, romance, science fiction, or horror story. If you are writing a story with a historical setting or one that is based on a true story, be sure you have studied the facts. The more you know the history, the more real your story will seem.

2 Create a story map. List major characters, a setting, and a theme. Then outline the plot (the most important events) of the story.

3 Write a rough draft.

(See also Rough Draft to Final Copy, p. 74.)

Just What Kind of Prose Story Is It?

Glossary of Fiction Forms

Although some stories are difficult to describe, others fit neatly into standard categories:

Allegory
A story in which the characters stand for ideas such as Love, Pride, Greed, or Tolerance. The plot usually has a message or moral about real life.

Fable
Like an allegory but short, with fewer characters and a simple moral. Aesop, a writer in ancient Greece, is probably the best-known *fabulist*, or writer of fables.

Fairy Tale
An adventure in which the heroes are often royalty or beloved by royalty and the villains are evil witches, sorcerers, or monsters.

Fantasy
A tale set in an imaginary world with imaginary characters. For example, animals can talk and fairies roam the countryside in fantasies.

Historical Fiction
Stories based on history, with fictional main characters. Historical fiction is sometimes set in real places and includes real people among its characters.

Horror
Tales about scary things, from ghosts and goblins to monsters and murderers.

Informational Fiction
A story or book that uses fictional characters or settings to tell about real things. For example, a story that explains science experiments might be told by a science teacher working in a fictional lab.

Legend
An exaggerated story about a real person or event. For example, there is a story that George Washington, our first president, could never tell a lie.

Mystery
Stories in which a problem is created by an unknown element. Mysteries are often crime stories. The main characters in mysteries are frequently detectives searching for a solution.

Myth
A story made up to explain real events. Myths help us understand the beliefs and everyday life of the people described in them. Myths once were used to answer difficult questions, such as how the moon and stars were created, why the seasons change, why the leopard has spots, etc. They also explained the relationships of human beings and gods. Almost every culture in the world has its own set of myths.

Realistic Fiction
Stories with imaginary characters and events that are so believable that they could take place in the real world.

Romance
Stories in which the main character or characters are looking for love and happiness. Some romances are historical and share many features of historical fiction.

Science Fiction
Stories, often set in the future, that use elements of modern science. Some science fiction stories are set on other planets. Others tell of aliens landing on Earth or of computers that run the world.

Tall Tales
Humorous stories that are full of exaggeration. Tall tales may or may not be about real people or events.

True Adventure
Stories based on real people or real events, but the plot, setting, and characters are partly made up by the author.

3 Writing Plays

Forms of Plays

A play is a story that is meant to be acted out. Like fiction, plays have characters, plots, and settings; beginnings, middles, and ends. The main difference is that, in a play, the story is told in dialogue and through the actions seen on a stage (which are written into the play as stage directions).

 *The author of a play is called a **playwright**. Some plays are short. Short plays are usually performed in one act and are called one-act plays. Longer plays consist of two or three acts.*

Acts are like the chapters in a book. In performances, acts are usually separated by breaks called *intermissions*. In plays of more than one act, the first act is called *Act I*, the second act *Act II*, etc. In most plays, acts are divided into *scenes*. Scenes often require changes in time, setting, or characters on the stage. Scenes are numbered with small Roman numerals. The first scene in the second act of a play, for example, is written *Act II*, *scene i*, or *II, i*.

The Day the Ice Cream Truck Broke Down

Act I, scene i: Lights come up to show Jeff and Jamal sitting on a curb, their bikes resting beside them. They are dressed in summer clothes; a cap is backward on Jamal's head. Both boys look hot and tired.

Jeff: Some ride. I could really use a soda! Let's go to my house and get something to drink.

Jamal: I can't move—not even for soda. (Jamal takes off his cap, wipes sweat from his forehead with his other hand, replaces cap.) Gotta rest, Jeff, gotta rest.

DRAMA:
A Brief History

Greek Drama

No one knows for certain when drama began. But we do know that more than 2,000 years ago, the Greeks presented powerful dramas that are still performed today.

In Greek theater, all the actors were men. Rather than use makeup, wigs, and costumes, the actors wore masks to fit their characters. Greek dramas also included a group of actors who stood on the side of the stage and chanted their reactions to the story. This group was called the chorus.

Passion Plays

In the Middle Ages (800–1400), passion plays, dramas about the death of Jesus, were very popular in Europe. In addition to passion plays, other stories from the Bible were acted out, often in the town square on market days.

Shakespearean Theater

By the 1500s, the Bible was no longer the main source for play ideas. Historical plays and dramas about everyday life were also acted out.

Globe Theatre

Probably the most important play-wright of this new era was William Shakespeare (1564–1616). In addition to writing 36 plays, he also built the Globe Theatre at Stratford-upon-Avon in England, the model for theaters ever since.

Chinese Theater

The theater in China took shape under the Yuan dynasty (1279–1368). The best-known form of drama today is the Beijing Opera, which became popular at the end of the 18th century. It combines dialogue and songs with dance, symbolic gestures, and acrobatics. The plays are based on Chinese history and folklore.

Japanese Theater

Not all dramas are acted out by using dialogue. Japanese *Noh* drama combines music and movement to tell a story. There is almost no scenery on the stage, and the actors wear masks and often elaborate costumes.

Other Forms of Drama

Mime is a dramatic form that uses movement and no dialogue to tell a story. *Operas* are dramas in which the characters sing the dialogue rather than speak it. *Musical theater* combines elements of plays with elements of opera, so that characters speak and sing their roles. *Puppet theater* uses puppets instead of people to portray the characters in the play.

Writing a Play

1 Decide what you want your play to be about.

2 Create a story map. Choose characters, a setting, and a plot outline. Will your play have one, two, or three acts?

3 Write a rough draft of your play. Don't worry about the exact dialogue. Instead, write down the action and the main idea, what the characters are saying to each other, and the setting and mood of the story.

4 When you're pleased with the rough draft, write precise dialogue and stage directions.

5 Read your play out loud. How does the dialogue sound to you? To a listener?

(See also Rough Draft to Final Copy, p. 74.)

Stage directions explain the setting and mood of a scene in a play. They also provide clues as to how the props, sets, and costumes should appear.

Scribing a Script:

Writing Down Dialogue and Stage Directions

The Day the Ice Cream Truck Broke Down

Act I, scene i: Lights come up to show Jeff and Jamal sitting on a curb, their bikes resting beside them. They are dressed in summer clothes; a cap is backward on Jamal's head. Both boys look hot and tired.

Jeff: Some ride. I could really use a soda! Let's go to my house and get something to drink.

Jamal: I can't move—not even for soda. (Jamal takes off his cap, wipes sweat from his forehead with his other hand, replaces cap.) Gotta rest, Jeff, gotta rest.

Dialogue in a play is written by showing the name of the speaker first, followed by a colon:

Following the name of the speaker is the line or lines a character is to say.

95

PRACTICAL WRITING

1 Journals

The word *journal* comes from the Latin word *diurnalis*, which means day. A journal is another name for a *daily diary*, a day-by-day account of events. Some people do write in their journals every day, but you may decide to write less often, for example, once a week or whenever you feel you have something important to say.

Keeping a Journal

1 Decide if you want to keep a journal in which you write about your feelings and thoughts or one in which you record major events, or both.

2 Write the date at the top of the page.

3 Write down the most important things that happened on that day. You might want to explain why you think the events are important.

4 Every so often, review what you've written in your journal. You may want to continue or expand your thoughts on a particular day, or you may want to note how your thoughts and feelings may have changed.

May 31

Dear Diary,
Only two more weeks of school! I can hardly wait for summer vacation—no more pencils, no more books...
Mel and I got in an argument today. It was pretty stupid, but we patched it up. Mr. Hatcher gave us an assignment that included cutting pictures from magazines. I couldn't do it because Mel had my scissors. So I whispered to Mel to give them back. Mr. Hatcher told me to be quiet. Then I raised my hand, but Mr. Hatcher wouldn't call on me. Anyway, I told Mel off at recess and then he got mad. After a while I felt bad. He's more important than scissors!

Letters

The ABCs of Letters

Letters come in two basic forms. *Formal*, or *business, letters* ask for and provide information. These letters are usually sent to strangers or acquaintances. *Personal letters* are sent between friends and relatives.

All letters have five basic parts:

1 Heading.
A heading includes the date, your address, and, in a formal letter, the name and address of the person to whom you are writing.

2 Greeting.
A greeting is a quick hello to the person receiving the letter. It usually begins with Dear. Be sure to capitalize the first letter in each word of the greeting. Put a comma at the end of the greeting in a personal letter, a colon in a business letter.

3 Body.
The body is the main part of the letter. Many people indent the first line of the body. If you indent the first line, then indent the first line of every paragraph in the letter.

4 Closing.
In a business letter, a closing can be Yours truly, Sincerely, or Regards. In a personal letter, you can write a familiar closing, for example, Your friend, Affectionately, or Love. Be sure to capitalize the first word of the closing and put a comma at the end of the closing.

5 Signature.
Always sign your letter below the closing. In a formal letter, be sure to print or type your name beneath your signature.

Writing a Formal Letter

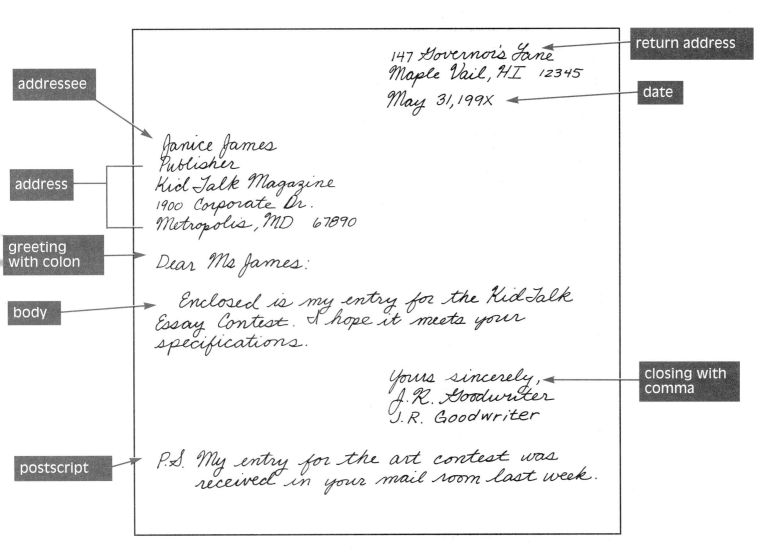

return address
147 Governor's Lane
Maple Vail, HI   12345

date
May 31, 199X

addressee

address
Janice James
Publisher
Kid Talk Magazine
1900 Corporate Dr.
Metropolis, MD   67890

greeting with colon
Dear Ms James:

body
Enclosed is my entry for the Kid Talk Essay Contest. I hope it meets your specifications.

closing with comma
Yours sincerely,
J. R. Goodwriter
J. R. Goodwriter

postscript
P.S. My entry for the art contest was received in your mail room last week.

Addressing an Envelope

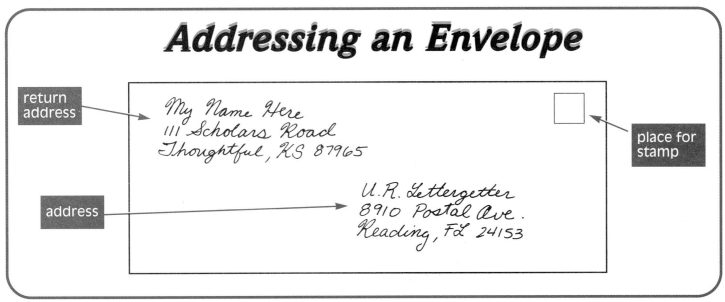

return address
My Name Here
111 Scholars Road
Thoughtful, KS 87965

place for stamp

address
U. R. Lettergetter
8910 Postal Ave.
Reading, FL 24153

Writing a Personal Letter

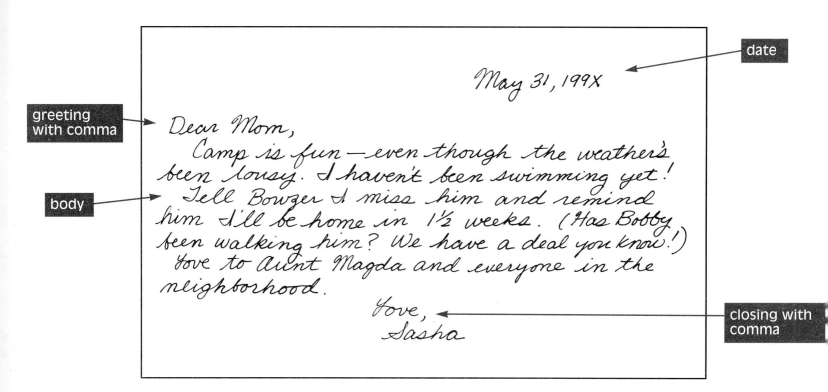

date

May 31, 199X

greeting with comma

Dear Mom,

Camp is fun — even though the weather's been lousy. I haven't been swimming yet!

body

Tell Bowzer I miss him and remind him I'll be home in 1½ weeks. (Has Bobby been walking him? We have a deal you know!)

Love to Aunt Magda and everyone in the neighborhood.

Love,
Sasha

closing with comma

A Party?
Writing Invitations

Invitations can be written on sheets of folded paper or on little squares of card stock. They can be formal or casual, colorful or plain. But invitations should always include four pieces of information:

1. Type of event (birthday party, surprise party, holiday theme party, costume party, club meeting, and so on)
2. Time
3. Date
4. Place

If you're serving food, you might want to add *R.S.V.P.* to the invitations. R.S.V.P. stands for *répondez s'il vous plaît,* and means "please respond." If you add R.S.V.P. be sure to supply a phone number or address so invitees will know how to respond.

Type of Event : Birthday

Time : 6:00 PM

Date : Saturday, June 10th

Place : Susan's house
123 Deer Run

R.S.V.P : 555·1234

Essays

Essays express personal opinions. You can write an essay about any topic or theme that you feel strongly about. Your essay may describe your feelings about the quality of food in the school cafeteria or why you love summer camp. Anything that stirs your emotions is probably a good essay topic.

To write an effective essay, you have to describe your opinions and ideas so that your readers can understand them. It's not enough to say that the food is awful or that camp is terrific. You need to back up your opinion with details so your readers will understand your point of view. You can use argument, humor, or exaggeration to make your points.

Writing an Essay

1 Choose a topic.

2 Outline the major points of your opinion
(see Outlines, pp. 66–67.)

3 Write a rough draft of your essay. The introduction should state the topic of your essay and your opinion on the topic. The body should list the reasons you feel as you do about your topic and offer any additional information or experiences to support your opinion. The conclusion should summarize the reasons you listed in the body of your essay and persuade your readers to share your opinion.

(See Rough Draft to Final Copy, p. 74.)

 Be sure to choose an essay topic that's manageable. For example, rather than write about "Sports and Kids," consider writing about "The Pressure on Kids to Win at Sports."

4 **Reports**

Reports are factual compositions. They describe the facts about anything—events, places, people, animals, plants, planets, stars, products, and more.

Writing a Report

1 Choose a topic.

2 Gather a variety of resource and reference material. Be sure you can find enough information to use in your report. If you find too much information, narrow down the subject of your report.

3 Take notes. As you read through the reference and resource material, write down the most important information and interesting facts. Be sure to keep track of the information and its sources. You'll need this for the bibliography (see p. 104).

4 Write an outline (see Outlines, pp. 66–67). Put all the information and interesting facts from your notes into an organized framework.

5 Write a rough draft. Incorporate as much information as you can from your outline and notes. The introduction should tell the topic of your report. The body should include important information and interesting facts. The conclusion should summarize the main points from the body.

6 Revise your report. Be sure the information in each of the paragraphs belongs together. Check to see that one paragraph flows smoothly into the next.

(See Rough Draft to Final Copy, p. 74.)

Using the Library to Research Your Report

You might have an encyclopedia at home or some books you can use to gather information for a report. But chances are you need to find additional material—so you go to the library. But how do you find the information you need in all those shelves of books? By using the card catalog.

The card catalog in most libraries is make up of index cards sorted into three categories:

1. **Subject cards**
2. **Author cards**
3. **Title cards**

Within each category, cards are sorted alphabetically in drawers. If you know the author of a book you need for research, go to the author drawers. If you know the title, try the title drawers. If you don't know an author or title, you can find information by looking up the subject you're interested in. Just go to the subject drawers.

In some libraries, the catalog is kept on computer. You simply search through the computer files by subject, author, and title.

REVIEWS:

Cross Between Essay and Report

Reviews combine ingredients of both essays and reports to give the facts—and then express an opinion.

Book reports are one kind of review. When you write a book report, you summarize the main events of the story and describe the characters, setting, and plot. You can describe the things you like or dislike about the book, as long as you make it clear that you're stating your opinion.

Reviews are written every day about everything from cars to toys, movies to music. Look in your local newspaper. You'll probably find a review or two there.

NONFICTION: Getting Real

Nonfiction takes on different forms and different topics, depending on the writer and the reasons for writing. Some reports fill entire books, or fulfill a particular purpose. These special reports have special names.

Autobiography   A story of the author's life.

Biography   A story of a person's life written by another person.

Essay   A nonfiction story that discusses one topic or theme from a personal point of view (see. p. 101).

History   An account of a past event or era.

Journal   A diary or record of day-to-day events (see p. 96).

News Stories   Reports written in a special format, usually used in newspapers and magazines (see. p. 106).

Reference   A collection of useful facts and information organized for quick study rather than for leisurely reading.

Travelogue   Nonfiction writing, often in the style of a journal or a news story, that tells about a journey or trip to a particular place.

Bibliography

A *bibliography* shows where you got the information for a report. It is a list of articles, books, or other sources.
   Bibliographies are organized alphabetically by the author's last name or, when there is no author named, by the name of the publication. Then the title is listed, followed by the name of the publisher. The place and date of publication are listed at the end.

Book Title

Publisher

Author

Anderson, Ariadne, <u>Those Wily Foxes</u>. School Books Press, New Freedom, Virginia, 1995.

Pub Date

Mehta, Suresh, "Fox Hunt: Foxes and Food," <u>Natural Life Magazine</u>. Cheeseboro, Vermont, March 1995.

Article Title

<u>World Wonders Encyclopedia</u>, Pine Mountain, Utah, 1992.

Publication Title

Better Book Reports:
A Seven-Step Plan

Getting Started

1 Select a book that interests you. Look at the cover.
Then read the title and the description on the book cover. If the book still seems interesting, open it. Are there pictures? Read a paragraph or two. Are you still interested? If not, try another book.

2 Read the book—all of it.

Getting Down to Business

3 Take notes for the first draft of your book report.
Write down the title, author, and genre (novel, history, biography, and so on) of the book. Then note the names of the major characters and the setting. Next, take notes on the main events, the problem (or conflict) in the book, and its solution. Last, describe one or two favorite episodes from the book.

4 Organize your notes and start your first draft.
Write down the title and author of the story. Then, write a one- to three-paragraph summary of the book. Don't retell every little detail or episode. Instead, limit your summary to the most important events in the story. Next, describe the problem or conflict in the story and how that problem is solved. This is especially important in writing a book report on a novel or piece of fiction. Last, give your opinion of the story and why you feel the way you do.

5 Read over your draft.
Try reading it aloud, and ask a friend or family member to read it, too. Note the parts that you want to revise.

Finishing Up

6 Edit your book report.
Reread your edited draft. Are you happy with it? Should you revise it even more, or are you satisfied with your work?

7 When you're finished with your draft, write a neat, final copy of your book report.

Fancy Thoughts

You may want to draw a picture of a scene from the book to include with the report. You might create an illustrated cover or choose to display your book report on a poster with several drawings. Perhaps you'd like to create a filmstrip about the book, one that includes your report and a series of illustrations for each part. Be creative!

5 News Stories

News stories are factual stories that usually have a special structure called a *pyramid*. The structure is called a pyramid because the first part of the story tells just the main facts. Then, as the story continues, the facts are described in greater detail to "widen" the story gradually to its "base," or conclusion. A good news story answers the questions *who, what, when, where, how,* and sometimes *why*.

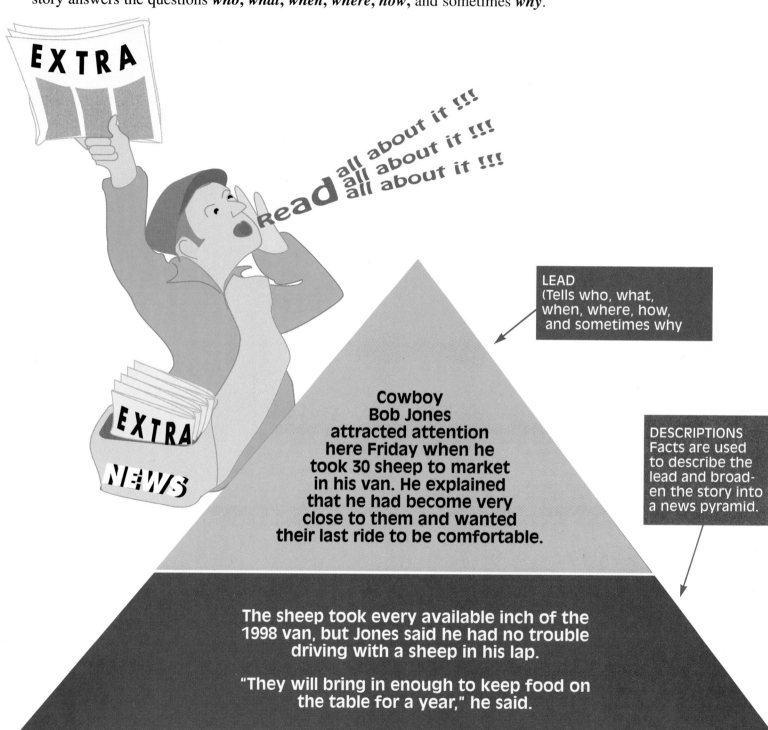

EXTRA

Read all about it !!!
all about it !!!
all about it !!!

EXTRA NEWS

LEAD
(Tells who, what, when, where, how, and sometimes why

Cowboy Bob Jones attracted attention here Friday when he took 30 sheep to market in his van. He explained that he had become very close to them and wanted their last ride to be comfortable.

DESCRIPTIONS
Facts are used to describe the lead and broaden the story into a news pyramid.

The sheep took every available inch of the 1998 van, but Jones said he had no trouble driving with a sheep in his lap.

"They will bring in enough to keep food on the table for a year," he said.

EXTRA! EXTRA!
READ ALL ABOUT IT!

asthead

hoto ustration

STUDENT NEWS

Volume 1, No. 1

Mid-November Edition

Headline

Caption

Unwelcome boosters spotted at pep rally

Bats Cause Queasy Feelings at Palmerston Pep Rally

Dateline

Oct. 31.- Bats are living in the Palmerston Elementary gym, according to maintenance engineer I. M. Scarett, who discovered the bats this morning. "There must be 50 or so hanging right behind the stage curtain on the north side of the gym," he reported. Scarett's discovery explains the moving shadows and odd whooshing noises reported in the gym at the evening pep rally on October 28.

Following the rally, student and teacher pep club members asked Palmerston maintenance to investigate the peculiar atmosphere in the gym.

"I sensed an odd presence," 5th grader Sarah Chandler remarked, "and heard kind of a low, beating sound, kind of a 'whoosh, whoosh' sound."

Amar Turk, a 4th grader, added, "The lights were weird. Shadows kept crossing the gym floor. But when I looked up, I didn't see anything. Just more shadows!"

Maintenance director Euby Comfort at first suspected the eerie effects were caused by a problem in the air circulation system. But Scarett, while investigating the air ducts on the gym stage, discovered a more likely culprit.

"Those bats were probably flying around behind the sheer stage curtain the night of the rally," Comfort concluded. Scarett added, "That sure would make one scary shadow play!"

Presley President

Headline

J. R. Presley clobbered the competition in the student council presidential election held last Tuesday, Election Day. Presley won 73 percent of the votes cast by Palmerston Elementary students.

Longer Lunch

Cutline

Presley attributes her landslide victory to her "longer lunch" platform.

"Our lunch period was cut this year from 20 minutes to 15. It's tough to get your lunch from the cafeteria line, take your seat, eat, and bus your tray in that time," Presley said.

In her campaign speech, Presley promised to negotiate with Principal McSwiney to restore the lost five minutes to the lunch schedule for all grades.

Index

Writing a News Story

1 Gather facts.
Be sure you can answer the questions *who*, *what*, *when*, *where*, and *how*. Take notes. If possible, interview people who are involved in the story or who are experts on your subject. Be sure you write down the exact words of the people you plan to quote.

2 Write a lead.
A lead is the first sentence or paragraph in a news story. Think of it as the tip of the pyramid. It tells the basic ideas of the story and gets the reader interested.

3 Write the body of the story.
The body fills in details about the lead.

4 Write a headline for your story.
Try to make the headline a catchy title, one that hints at the action in the news story.

1 Expressions

Expressions are words or phrases that are used to convey ideas or feelings beyond their dictionary definitions. Expressions color our thoughts and ideas and provide writers with a shortcut to explaining a complex concept or feeling. Some expressions relate ideas to historical events or people, others to myths, legends, or the Bible.

Many authors use expressions in their books and articles. That means you need to understand the expressions in order to understand their writing.

Adages, Proverbs, and Maxims

Adages, proverbs, and maxims are sayings that have been used for many years that tell truths about life or human nature. For example:

A stitch in time saves nine.

If you sew up a tear when it requires only one stitch to fix, the tear won't get bigger and require a greater effort — nine stitches — to fix later. This expression means that if you pay attention to problems and solve them early, they won't become bigger problems later on.

Clichés

Clichés are sayings that have been used too much to make a strong impression. Clichés should be avoided in writing and speaking. For example:

That person is as odd as a three-dollar bill.

Because there is no such thing as a three-dollar bill, the person is odd or silly.

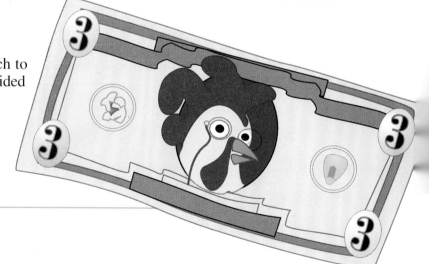

Expressions from History, Literature, and the Bible

Achilles' heel   A weak spot. In Greek mythology, Achilles was a hero whose only weak spot was on his heel. He was unbeatable in battle until an arrow finally struck him in the heel.

In school, math was his Achilles' heel.

Add insult to injury   Make a bad situation worse. In a fable by Aesop (see p. 91), a man swats at a fly that has bitten him on his head. Instead of hitting the fly, he hits himself on his sore head. The fly muses that the man has "added insult to injury" by making more pain for himself unnecessarily.

By insisting he was not stealing when he was caught with the merchandise, John simply added insult to injury.

Baker's dozen   Thirteen, or a little extra. This expression dates back to 1266 in England. Laws were passed by Parliament to protect people from bakers who offered small loaves of bread. To ensure that they met the government standards for weight, the bread bakers threw in an extra loaf per dozen (or 12) sold.

He gave me a baker's dozen of cupcakes.

Cry wolf   Call for help when there's no danger. About 2,500 years ago, Aesop wrote a story about a shepherd boy who was protecting a flock of sheep from a wolf. The boy was bored and decided to call out as if the wolf were threatening the sheep. Maybe someone would come. So he cried, "Wolf!" Sure enough, the village people came running to help the boy protect the sheep. When they discovered the wolf was not around, they were annoyed and returned home. But as the days went by, the boy grew more bored and again cried, "Wolf!" The villagers came again and were even more annoyed when they found the boy was bluffing. They went home. Then one day the wolf really did come. The boy called out, "Wolf! Wolf!" But no one came. The villagers thought he was bluffing. The moral: If you keep telling lies, no one will believe you, even when you tell the truth!

He's always crying wolf, so I can't believe he really has a headache.

Drop in the bucket   An amount that doesn't matter. In the Bible, the prophet Isaiah explains that God has created a vast universe. He continues to say that the nations of the world are but drops in the bucket by comparison—unimportant.

This worksheet is a drop in the bucket compared with the three tests coming up next week!

Eat humble pie   Apologize for making an error. The original expression was to eat *umble* pie. Umble—the heart, liver, and intestines of deer—used to be cooked up in pies for poor people while the wealthy enjoyed the loins and ribs of the animal.

When she proved I was wrong, I ate humble pie.

Go whole hog   Stop at nothing. Eating pork was against the religious laws of Judaism and Islam, although religious scholars often puzzled over whether it was only certain parts of the hog that could not be eaten. To go whole hog was to forget about the laws and splurge.

I sure went whole hog when I spent all my allowance on that game cartridge!

Idioms

Idioms are sayings whose meanings can't be understood from the individual words in them. For example:

Apple of one's eye. The "apple of one's eye" is not an apple in a person's eye. It is a favorite person. The idiom comes from the idea that an apple is a beautiful thing to see and promises to hold good things inside. A favorite person is always pleasant to see and well-loved—that is, good inside.

Herbert's daughter, Wendy, is the apple of his eye.

Greek to me. Too difficult to understand. In the Shakespeare play *Julius Caesar*, the Romans speak Greek when they want to keep their messages secret. One of the Romans, a fellow named Casca, is asked if he'd heard some important news. He says, ". . . for mine part, it was Greek to me." Casca had no idea what was said.

My sister studies algebra, but it's Greek to me.

In the doghouse In trouble and being punished. In *Peter Pan*, Mr. Darling treats Nana harshly. His children are angry with him, so he sits in Nana's doghouse until they'll speak to him again.

Dom has been in the doghouse with Mom ever since he left his new bike in the rain.

John Hancock Your signature. John Hancock was an American patriot and first signer of the Declaration of Independence. He wrote his name especially large at the bottom of the Declaration to make sure it could be seen.

They put their John Hancocks on the petition to save the whales.

Mad as a hatter. Crazy. Hatters, or milliners, used mercury to treat the felt fabric used for hats. The mercury gave many of the hatters a severe twitch, which made it impossible for them to work, much less act normally. The Mad Hatter is a well-known character in *Alice's Adventures in Wonderland*.

Stay away from that guy. He's mad as a hatter.

(Open) Pandora's box Ask for trouble. In Greek mythology, Pandora was given a box by Zeus, who told her she must never open it because it contained everything bad in the world—illness, sadness, gloom, and misery. But curiosity got the best of Pandora. She opened the box and released all the ills on the world.

When the principal asked for criticisms, she really opened Pandora's box.

Read between the lines Guess at the real meaning of things, or the truth behind what is written. Before paper was common, books and official documents were written on parchment made from animal skins. Parchment was very valuable. Rather than throw it away if the messages on it were old, it was reused. The old ink was covered over to make a clear page for another document. On some old parchment, you can actually "read between the lines" because the writing underneath shows through.

She said the rock star was out of the country, but, if you read between the lines, she probably was just saying that so he wouldn't have to talk to reporters.

Slow and steady wins the race Aesop's fable "The Tortoise and the Hare" tells about a race between a tortoise and a hare (rabbit). The hare teases the tortoise, but the tortoise keeps going. The hare is so confident that he will win the race that he stops for a nap. As he sleeps, the tortoise, slowly but surely, crosses the finish line first.

Chonra studied a little every night last week for her social studies test. Kendra crammed the night before. Kendra wrote ten wrong answers, and Chonra wrote only one. Slow and steady wins the race.

Sour grapes Fools dislike what they cannot have. In Aesop's fable "The Fox and the Grapes," a fox passes a vineyard and spies some tasty-looking grapes. He jumps the fence and tries to grasp the grapes in his jaw, but they are out of reach. The fox tries again and again, but still cannot claim the prized grapes. At last the fox stomps off toward home, saying, "Who needs those grapes? They're probably sour anyway."

After Ferdie's team lost the soccer match, he said the other team cheated, but I think it was just sour grapes.

Wolf in sheep's clothing Someone or something that isn't what it appears to be. In an Aesop fable, a wolf puts on a sheepskin in order to blend in with a flock of sheep—the easier to kill the sheep for his supper. But the shepherd has the last laugh. He thinks the wolf is a sheep and kills him for his own supper.

K. C. said she was joining our team because she liked us better, but I'm afraid she may be a wolf in sheep's clothing.

APPENDIX
SOME GOOD BOOKS TO READ

FICTION

Adventure

Call It Courage
by Armstrong Sperry
A Polynesian chief's son proves his manhood by conquering his fear of the sea in a voyage to a distant island. Macmillan Children's Books.

The Call of the Wild
by Jack London
After a series of savage adventures and the loss of a loving master, Buck — part Saint Bernard, part shepherd dog — returns to the wild as leader of a wolf pack. Scholastic Apple Classic.

Slake's Limbo
by Felice Holman
The story of a homeless 13-year-old boy and how he survives in a niche under Grand Central Station in New York City. Macmillan Children's Group.

Spirit Quest
by Susan Sharpe
Aaron and his new friend Robert, a Quileute boy, find adventure on a Spirit Quest, a Quileute wilderness experience. Macmillan Children's Group.

Fantasy and Science Fiction

Aliens in the Family
by Margaret Mahy
An alien boy named Bond becomes the "bond" between alienated stepsiblings. Scholastic Hardcover.

The Black Pearl
by Scott O'Dell
Ramon found the fabulous Pearl of Heaven, but all it earned him was powerful enemies. Houghton Mifflin.

The Book of Three
by Lloyd Alexander
Young Taran and his odd assortment of companions set out to save the mythical kingdom from the forces of evil. H. Holt and Co.

The Cat Who Went to Heaven
by Elizabeth Coatsworth
A poor Japanese artist's new cat, Good Fortune, seems to bring him good luck. The artist is commissioned to paint a scroll of the death of Buddha, but his luck begins to fade when he paints Good Fortune onto the scroll. Macmillan Children's Books.

The Deadly Power of Medusa
by Mary Pope and Will Osborne
A thrilling retelling of the quest for the head of Medusa, a mythical monster with hair of snakes and a gaze that turned men to stone. Scholastic Apple Classic.

Favorite Greek Myths
by Mary Pope Osborne
A handsome, distinctive volume of twelve ancient Greek stories made exciting and accessible for today's readers. Scholastic Inc.

Five Children and It
by E. Nesbit
The lives of five children are turned upside down when they discover a wish-granting creature. Scholastic Paperback.

Folklore, Fairy Tales, and Legends and Aesop's Fables
by Ann McGovern
Timeless classics retold in modern language. Scholastic Apple Classic.

The Golden Goblet
by Eloise Jarvis McGraw
Ranofer struggles to thwart his evil brother's plot so he can become a master goldsmith like their father. An exciting tale of ancient Egyptian mystery and intrigue. Puffin Books.

The Listening Silence
by Phyllis Root
This story, inspired by Native American mythology, is about a young orphaned girl named Kiri who has a special gift of healing. She is cared for by Mali, an elderly healer. Kiri, not wanting to follow Mali's path, sets out on her own. HarperCollins Children's Books.

Peter Pan
by J. M. Barrie
The unabridged, timeless classic about a magical place called Neverland and a boy who won't grow up. Scholastic Apple Classic.

The Phantom Tollbooth
by Norton Juster
Milo embarks on an exciting adventure in a strange country of edible words and mysterious creatures as he visits the Kingdom of Wisdom, Dictionopolis, and the Mountains of Ignorance. Knopf Books for Young Readers.

In the Year of the Boar and Jackie Robinson
by Betty Bao Lord
A young Chinese girl emigrates to New York in 1947 and encounters a strange new culture of school-yard toughs, stickball games, and the Brooklyn Dodgers. HarperCollins Children's Books.

Journey to Jo'burg: A South African Story
by Beverly Naidoo
When their baby sister becomes seriously ill, Naledi and Tiro must travel to Johannesburg to find their mother. Their journey becomes a lesson in apartheid. HarperCollins Children's Books.

The Land I Lost: Adventures of a Boy in Vietnam
by Huynh Quang Nhuong
A fictionalized memoir of the people, customs, and animals of a boyhood spent in a small Vietnamese village. HarperCollins Children's Books.

The Legend of Jimmy Spoon
by Kristiana Gregory
Kidnapped by Shoshoni, 12-year-old Jimmy adjusts to their Native American way of life. Inspired by a true story, this is a compelling tale of adventure and coming of age. Harcourt Brace.

Little Women
by Louisa May Alcott
The beloved classic about the four lovely March sisters who grew up in New England a century ago. Scholastic Apple Classic.

The Long Winter
by Laura Ingalls Wilder
The Ingalls live in Pa's store in town during the terrible winter of 1880–1881. The story of those long, dangerous months is filled with historical details and scenes of family life. HarperCollins Children's Books.

Midnight Is a Place
by Joan Aiken
The acclaimed author of **The Wolves of Willoughby Chase** tells the exciting adventure of two orphans struggling to survive in 19th-century England. Dell.

My Daniel
by Pam Conrad
An old woman tells her granddaughter how her beloved teenage brother, Daniel, was destroyed at the time of the frenzied hunt for dinosaur remains in Nebraska before the turn of the century. HarperCollins Children's Books.

The Perilous Road
by William O. Steele
An engrossing, realistic story of a Tennessee mountain boy who, during the Civil War, comes to realize that war is terrible no matter where one's sympathies lie. Harcourt Brace.

Sarah, Plain and Tall
by Patricia MacLachlan
Two children experience the apprehensions and joys of the possibility of a new mother when their father invites a mail-order bride to their prairie home. HarperCollins Children's Books.

Sounder
by William H. Armstrong
A compelling story of a boy's tenacity for life in an African-American sharecropper family. A tale of courage, human dignity, and love. HarperCollins Children's Books.

The Star Fisher
by Lawrence Yep
A moving portrayal of the struggle of a young Chinese-American girl and her family as they fight for respect in a small West Virginia town during the late 1920s. Morrow Junior Books.

Steal Away
by Jennifer Armstrong
Two girls — one African-American, one white — escape North together during the Civil War. Orchard Books, Watts.

Realistic Fiction

Angela and the Broken Heart
by Nancy K. Robinson
When Angela's teenage brother falls for a girl who does not return his affections, Angela concocts an inventive plan to help him. The plan backfires with comically touching results. Scholastic Hardcover.

Arthur for the Very First Time
by Patricia MacLachlan
When Arthur, a ten-year-old boy set in his ways, visits his aunt and uncle's farm, he learns to see, think, and feel things he never has before. HarperCollins Children's Books.

Black Beauty
Anna Sewell
The beloved classic about the life and hard times of a magnificent thoroughbred stallion. Scholastic Apple Classic.

The Blind Colt
by Glen Rounds
A wild colt that was born blind learns how to survive on the open range. Holiday.

Bridge to Terabithia
by Katherine Paterson
Jess and Leslie create their own kingdom in the woods until tragedy strikes and one of them must face life alone. HarperCollins Children's Books.

The Broccoli Tapes
by Jan Slepian
Sara discovers the value of love and friendship during her five-month stay in Hawaii. Putnam Publishing Group.

Bummer Summer
by Ann M. Martin
Kammy must cope with two new experiences in one summer: the remarriage of her widowed father and summer camp. Holiday.

The Burning Questions of Bingo Brown
by Betsy Byars
Eleven-year-old Bingo's life isn't easy, so he writes down all of his crazy questions and observations in a journal. Viking Children's Books.

Cassie Binegar
by Patricia MacLachlan
After her grandfather's death, Cassie longs for a life that's orderly and predictable. But during an eventful summer by the sea, she begins to learn that some things are not meant to stay the same. HarperCollins Children's Books.

The Cat Ate My Gymsuit
by Paula Danzinger
Marcy organizes a student protest on behalf of her suspended English teacher. Delacorte.

Class President
by Johanna Hurwitz
Julio discovers his leadership skills as the class prepares to hold an election for class president. Morrow Junior Books.

Dear Dad, Love Laurie
by Susan Beth Pfeffer
Laurie chronicles her sixth-grade year in weekly letters to her divorced father. Scholastic Paperback.

Dear Mr. Henshaw
by Beverly Cleary
Leigh Botts, the new kid in town, pours his heart out to his favorite author. Morrow Junior Books.

Five Little Peppers and How They Grew
by Margaret Sidney
The Peppers are the poorest people in town, but their devotion to each other makes them richer than anyone. Scholastic Paperback.

Freckle Juice
by Judy Blume
Andrew wants freckles more than anything else, so Sharon offers to sell him her secret freckle recipe. Dell.

Good-bye, My Wishing Star
by Vicki Grove
The poignant story of a young girl who experiences the pain of losing her family's farm. Scholastic Inc.

Henry and Ribsy
by Beverly Cleary
Henry can go salmon fishing with his father, but only on one condition: that he keep his dog Ribsy out of trouble for one month. Morrow Junior Books.

Justin and the Best Biscuits in the World
by Mildred Pitts Walter
An eccentric old cowboy teaches his lazy ten-year-old grandson how to do real "men's work." An exciting rodeo and a history of the African-American cowboys combine to create a very special story. Lothrop.

Misty of Chincoteague
by Marguerite Henry
Paul and Maureen capture and tame Phantom, a beautiful wild mare and her colt, Misty. Macmillan Children's Group.

Mom, You're Fired
by Nancy K. Robinson
A series of comic incidents helps ten-year-old Tina gain new appreciation for her "free-spirit" mother. Scholastic Inc.

Plain Girl
by Virginia Sorenson
A sensitive, perceptive book about a nine-year-old Amish girl who faces many problems when the authorities insist she go to public school. Harcourt Brace.

Sixth Grade Can Really Kill You
by Barthe DeClements
Helen is a likable practical joker. Her lack of self-control is partly due to a learning disability, but a sympathetic teacher helps her overcome her problems. Viking Children's Books.

The Summer of the Swans
by Betsy Byars
Sara's adolescent pains and problems fade when her mentally retarded brother, Charlie, disappears one night. Viking Children's Books.

Thank You, Jackie Robinson
by Barbara Cohen
The humorous, touching story of an unlikely friendship between two die-hard baseball fans. Lothrop.

NONFICTION

Biography

Bully for You, Teddy Roosevelt
by Jean Fritz
This lively biography captures the exuberance and enthusiasm of Teddy Roosevelt. Putnam Publishing Group.

Childtimes
by E. Greenfield and Leslie L. Little
In this lyrical memoir, three African-American women — a daughter, mother, and grandmother — bring to life again the children they once were and the times they used to have. Scholastic Paperback.

Colin Powell: A Biography
by Jim Haskins
Colin Powell, the first African-American Chairman of the Joint Chiefs of Staff and the man who oversaw Operation Desert Storm, comes to life. Scholastic Inc.

The First Woman Doctor
by Rachel Baker
An engrossing biography of Elizabeth Blackwell, the first female doctor, who founded a women's hospital and medical college. Scholastic Inc.

Frederick Douglass Fights for Freedom
by Margaret Davidson
Born a slave, Frederick Douglass went on to become one of the most famous freedom fighters of all time. Black-and-white photos. Scholastic Apple.

George Washington: The Man Who Would Not Be King
by Stephen Krensky
Readers learn how this modest man led the Revolution and later became the new nation's first president. Scholastic Inc.

Indian Chiefs
by Russell Freedman
Compelling profiles of six Indian chiefs who led their people in a historic crisis. With photos, a map, and an index. Dutton Children's Books.

Jesse Jackson: A Biography
by Patricia McKissack
The life and times of the noted civil rights activist and presidential candidate. Scholastic Hardcover.

Lost Star: The Story of Amelia Earhart
by Patricia Lauber
A fascinating look at the life of America's most famous female aviator. Scholastic Inc.

The Magic: Earvin Johnson
by Bill Morgan
The story of one of America's most-beloved basketball stars. This biography describes his life, emphasizing the qualities that have made him a leader on the courts, and those that will help him as a spokesperson for HIV prevention. Scholastic Inc.

Nelson Mandela: "No Easy Walk to Freedom"
by Barry Denenberg
The up-to-date story of Mandela's life, from his 26-year imprisonment to his recent release, and his visit to the United States. Black-and-white photos. Scholastic Hardcover.

Our 42nd President: Bill Clinton
by Jack Roberts
A fact-filled look at the life of William Jefferson Clinton, from his childhood until his election as our 42nd President. Scholastic Paperback.

Ready, Aim, Fire! The Real Adventures of Annie Oakley
by Ellen Levine
The biography of the western heroine Annie Oakley — the great sharpshooter who became a legend in her own time. Black-and-white photos. Scholastic Inc.

The Secret Soldier: The Story of Deborah Sampson
by Ann McGovern
The fascinating story of a young woman who disguised herself as a man and fought bravely during the Revolutionary War. Macmillan Children's Group.

So Young to Die: The Story of Hannah Senesh
by Candice F. Ransom
The compelling biography of a heroic young Jewish woman who escaped to Palestine during World War II, then returned to Europe to rescue others. Scholastic Paperback.

Stealing Home: The Story of Jackie Robinson
by Barry Denenberg
The biography of the first African-American major-league baseball player, whose courage in fighting for racial equality made him a great hero. Scholastic Inc.

The Story of Helen Keller
by Lorena Hickok
The courage and determination that made the deaf, mute, and blind girl an inspiration to people around the world illuminate this fine, detailed biography. Scholastic Paperback.

Thomas Jefferson: The Man with a Vision
by Ruth Crisman
This fascinating biography of our third president details his greatest achievements, such as the Declaration of Independence, and reveals his varied interests, including music and architecture. Scholastic Paperback.

What's the Big Idea, Ben Franklin?
by Jean Fritz
A lively biography of the eighteenth-century printer, inventor, and statesman. Putnam Publishing Group.

Where Was Patrick Henry on the 29th of May?
by Jean Fritz
An intriguing biography, stressing both the good and bad characteristics of Henry. Some of the facts are unusual and often humorous. Putnam Publishing Group.

Informational Books

Aircraft Carriers
by Michael Taylor
A fascinating look at the world of modern aircraft carriers, the planes, and the people who work onboard. Colorful photos. Scholastic Inc.

Birth of an Island
by Millicent E. Selsam
The noted science writer describes the evolution of an island. Scholastic Paperback.

Blood and Guts: A Working Guide to Your Own Insides
by Linda Allison
An excellent, lively explanation of how the body works. Jaunty illustrations. Little, Brown and Co.

Exploring the Titanic
by Robert D. Ballard
The story of the sinking and the discovery of the *Titanic* written by the man who discovered the famous shipwreck. With never-before-seen photos from the 1985 expedition. Scholastic Inc.

Fighters, Choppers, and Bombers
by Luke Begarnie
This concise pictorial guide to modern U.S. combat aircraft gives detailed information on the design and capabilities of fighter planes, helicopters, and bombers. Fascinating, colorful photographs show these aircraft performing maneuvers and in formation. Scholastic Inc.

How the White House Really Works
by George Sullivan
A photo-filled, guided tour of the White House, from the Oval Office to the kitchen — where thousands of pieces of china are hand washed every day — to the president's bowling alley. Scholastic Inc.

Looking Inside Machines and Constructions
by Paul Fleischer and Patricia Keeler
Did you ever wonder how your front door unlocks when you turn the right key? How an escalator generates a never-ending supply of steadily moving stairs? Every page in this book gives the reader a behind-the-scenes look at how things work. Macmillan Children's Group.

The Lost Wreck of the Isis
by Robert D. Ballard
The discovery and exploration of the remains of an ancient Roman shipwreck.
Scholastic Inc.

Protecting Endangered Species at the San Diego Zoo
by Georgeann Irving
It's difficult to imagine our world without such magnificent creatures as the
Galápagos tortoise, the black rhinoceros, the clouded leopard, and many other
endangered species, yet many have already disappeared and others soon may.
Learn what the San Diego Zoo and San Diego Wildlife Park are doing in their
endangered-species conservation efforts. Simon & Schuster Trade.

Radical Robots: Can You Be Replaced?
by George Harrar
Learn all about robots! This challenging book, full of facts and photos, is a
fascinating reference book. Simon & Schuster Trade.

The Secrets of Vesuvius: Exploring the Mysteries of an Ancient Buried City
by Sara C. Bisel
The archaeological exploration and history of Herculaneum, a Roman
town buried 2,000 years ago by the eruption of Mount Vesuvius.
Scholastic Hardcover.

The Story of the Ice Age
by Rose Wyler and Gerald Adams
The discovery of a strange beast, found frozen in Siberia in 1799, leads to the
study of the Ice Age. Scholastic Inc.

Totem Pole
by Diane Hoyt-Goldsmith
Photographed by Lawrence Migdale, David, a member of the Tsimshian tribe,
proudly talks about the craft of his father, a woodcarver. From face masks to
totem poles, David explains the steps and traditions that are involved in this
much-respected skill. Holiday.

Volcanoes and Earthquakes
by Patricia Lauber
All the latest scientific data about the natural phenomena of earthquakes and
volcanoes. More than 30 photos. Scholastic Inc.

What's Beyond? Solving Mysteries in Space
by Michael Cusack
A clear, up-to-date survey of space discoveries made during the last two
decades. NASA and other official photographs illustrate the indexed text.
Scholastic Paperback.

Who Really Discovered America?
by Stephen Krensky
This humorously told, informative book describes the arrivals in America of
Columbus's predecessors, from the Vikings to Asian nomads crossing a land
bridge to lost ships from China to India. Scholastic Inc.

Information with a Story

Dolphin Adventure: A True Story
by Wayne Grover
Against the background of a you-are-there description of the ocean's depths, readers relive the author's incredible but true encounter with a dolphin family. Greenwillow.

Rascal
by Sterling North
The true story of the author's boyhood, when he takes in Rascal — a mischievous, endearing raccoon — as a pet. Avon.

Sea Otter Rescue: The Aftermath of the Oil Spill
by Roland Smith
A firsthand, dramatic account of the attempts to rescue the sea otters of Prince William Sound after the 1989 Exxon Valdez oil spill. Dutton Children's Books.

Shh! We're Writing the Constitution
by Jean Fritz
The author documents the Constitutional Convention, bringing history to life. A copy of the Constitution is included. Putnam Publishing Group.

The Slave Ship
by Emma Gelders Sterne
The *Amistad*, a Caribbean schooner, was "pirated" by its slave passengers in 1839 in this gripping sea saga. Scholastic Inc.

Two Tickets to Freedom: The True Story of William and Ellen Craft, Fugitive Slaves
by Florence B. Freedman
The remarkable true story of a married couple who risked their lives, fleeing from slavery disguised as a white man and his slave. P. Bedrick Books.

Undying Glory
by Clinton Cox
The moving story of the courageous men of the 54th Regiment of Massachusetts, who fought as Union soldiers to free their brothers and sisters from slavery. Archive photographs bring the "glory" regiment to vivid life. Scholastic Inc.

Photoessay

The Day Martin Luther King, Jr., Was Shot: A Photo History of the Civil Rights Movement
by Jim Haskins
A stirring look at the history of the fight for civil rights and the gains made since the fateful day of King's death. With powerful photographs. Scholastic Inc.

The Day Pearl Harbor Was Bombed: A Photo History of World War II
by George Sullivan
The historic events that occured before, during, and after World War II presented in a contemporary magazine format. Includes an index, chronology, and front-page newspaper headlines. Scholastic Inc.

The Death of Lincoln: A Picture History of the Assassination
by Leroy Hayman
Here is a factual, detailed account of Lincoln's last days, his death, and what happened to the conspirators and the nation in the days that followed Lincoln's assassination. Scholastic Inc.

Immigrant Kids
by Russell Freedman
During the late 1800s and early 1900s, immigrant kids sold newspapers, hauled firewood, worked in sweatshops, and did many other kinds of work. After work, they played, fought rival gangs, and became integrated into American life. Illustrated with 50 authentic photos. Dutton Children's Books.

Prairie Visions: The Life and Time of Solomon Butcher
by Pam Conrad
You can experience the lives of Nebraska pioneers at the turn of the century through the eyes and photographs of a man named Solomon Butcher. HarperCollins Children's Books.

A Reef Comes to Life: Creating an Undersea Exhibit
by Nat Segaloff and Paul Erikson
Lively text and breathtaking, colorful photographs offer readers a behind-the-scenes look at how a coral reef is reconstructed into a dazzling exhibit for all to enjoy. Watts.

Space Camp
by Anne Baire
Each year thousands of children pour into the world-famous U.S. Space Camp to find out what it feels like to be a NASA astronaut. This book lets you become a part of that thrilling experience. Fifty dramatic photographs, and you-are-there text, follow a group of kids through their week-long training session, which includes a simulated space shuttle mission. Morrow Junior Books.

The Wright Brothers: How They Invented the Airplane
by Russell Freedman
Readers are introduced to the lives and high-flying achievements of Orville and Wilbur Wright. Fascinating photos taken by the Wrights and their contemporaries help document the journey. Scholastic Paperback.

tall tales, 91
tenses, 42, 43
  see specific tenses; verbs
theme, 64, 80, 101
time line, 71, 81
tone, 80
topic, 66, 80, 101
topic sentences, 64, 65
travelogue, 104
true adventure, 91

underline, 62
uppercase letters (see capital
  letters)

Venn diagram, 73, 81
verb phrases, 53
verbs, 41–43
  action, 41
  adverbs and, 46
  clauses, 54
  gerunds, 53
  helping, 41, 43
  infinitives, 42
  irregular, 43
  linking, 41
  participles, 43
  phrases, 52–53
  in predicates, 54, 55
  principal parts, 43
  regular, 43
  in sentences, 55
  suffixes and, 22
  tenses, 42, 43
vowels
  sounds, 15–18
  spelling rules, 24

W

writing
  bibliography, 104
  book reports, 105
  editing symbols, 75
  essays, 101
  evaluating, 81–85
  journals (diaries), 96–97
  letters, 98–100
  news stories, 106, 108
  plays, 94–95
  poetry, 89
  prewriting, 66–73
  prose stories, 90–91
  reports, 102, 103
  reviews, 103
  rough drafts, 74
  terms and techniques, 76–80
  stories, 90
  see also prewriting
writing systems, 9
  see also alphabets; sign and
    symbol languages

$8.95 US/ $12.99 CAN

SCHOLASTIC HOMEWORK REFERENCE SERIES
In collaboration with UFT DIAL-A-TEACHER

Need to know how to find the main idea? How to use a dictionary to find the meaning of a word? How to form a contraction? What a participle is? How to write a book report—or a poem?

Everything You Need to Know About English Homework provides fourth-to-sixth-grade students and their parents with the information they need to complete English assignments. With the help of Dial-A-Teacher, which has operated a telephone help line since 1979, the authors have compiled this English reference guide with easy-to-understand answers to students' most frequently asked questions. No other source offers such a full range of information directly related to the fourth through sixth grade English curriculum.

THE SCHOLASTIC HOMEWORK REFERENCE SERIES

Everything You Need to Know About American History Homework

Everything You Need to Know About English Homework

Everything You Need to Know About Geography Homework

Everything You Need to Know About Math Homework

Everything You Need to Know About Science Homework

Everything You Need to Know About World History Homework

Ages 9 and up

SCHOLASTIC REFERENCE
Scholastic Inc.
New York

ISBN 0-590-49361-2

50895

9 780590 493611